KNIVES
& knifemakers

KNIVES
& knifemakers

SID LATHAM

COLLIER BOOKS
A Division of Macmillan Publishing Co., Inc.
NEW YORK

COLLIER MACMILLAN PUBLISHERS
LONDON

To the American Knifemaker

Duo faciem idem
non est idem

Macmillan Publishing Co., Inc.
866 Third Avenue, New York, N. Y. 10022
Collier Macmillan Canada, Ltd.

Library of Congress Catalog Card Number: 73-78815

Knives and Knifemakers was published in a hardcover edition by
Winchester Press and is reprinted by agreement.

First Collier Books Edition 1974
Second Printing 1977
Printed in the United States of America

contents

acknowledgments

Many knifemakers were kind enough to answer endless letters, sit for interviews, lend knives and generally do what they could to educate this neophyte. Rod Chappel, Walter Collins, Dan Dennehy, Ted Dowell, Bob Dozier, Clyde Fischer, Lloyd Hale and Corbet Sigman were particularly helpful, and to all these men my wholehearted thanks are due. Without their support this book would not have been possible.

I owe a very special debt of gratitude to Andy Russell and Bob Loveless, respectively honorary president and founding secretary of the Knifemakers Guild. Both were generous with their time and patience during the long months of preparation, and both made invaluable suggestions and corrections to the manuscript's first draft.

Harry McEvoy provided me with important background information on William Scagel, whose close friend and unofficial biographer he was, and Bo Randall, Jr., lent me Scagel knives from his personal collection to photograph. To them, my sincere thanks.

Finally, I must thank my wife, Lilyan, who wistfully hopes that my next effort might be about precious stones.

—Sid Latham

New York, N.Y.
June 1973

foreword

Men who make knives and ship them to customers all over the country have been watching the growing popularity of their work during the past several years, often with surprise and wonder. Knifemakers who have been working for a dozen years and longer have always known of a certain narrow market for the knives, but the growth in just the last three or four years of collecting and field use has been startling.

Perhaps it is a small residual atavism, an almost subconscious awareness of the knife as tool, as weapon, and as object of pleasure that causes men to buy them and collect them. And perhaps it is the growing knowledge that the knife can be used every day, for so many jobs, while the rifle or shotgun must often remain on the wall waiting for an often-postponed field trip. And I think many outdoorsmen have come to know the knife, to become aware of the variety and richness of current work by modern knifemakers who nowadays offer knives of every shape and size and degree of richness in ornamentation.

Whatever the reasons, many knifemakers have begun to see the need for a basic book on the modern knife and the men who make them. Indeed, most of us prefer to work with intelligent, informed customers who know our work, our problems, and our areas of interest. Because modern knifemakers are a various breed, with major differences of viewpoint and method (and in fact of skills), a careful study of both the men and their work will repay the reader who plans to deal with one or more of us.

In any event, we've wanted this book, and when Sid Latham told me of his plans to write it, and then came to Kansas City to the Third Annual Business Meeting & Knife Show of the Knifemakers Guild to implement his plans, several of us met his interest with our own.

And it was soon evident that Sid planned no mere surface treatment of the subject. We sat in a hotel room one evening, and as we talked, trying to cover this complex subject in depth, it was obvious to me that he had in fact paid his dues. His continuing interest was genuine, and he was intent on learning his subject in detail. Two evenings later, Corbet Sigman and I sat and reasoned together into Sid's tape recorder, and I knew when I read that material in the book how faithfully Sid had learned to understand our work.

I've come to know Sid Latham well, this last pair of years. He has seen and done many things, and been many places. He and his work have earned my own respect, and I commend his book to all those many men (and a few women) who have gotten interested in knives and knifemakers, indeed to the many fine people who have supported me and my peers with their orders, with their unfailing courtesy and patience, and with the wherewithal for us to pursue maybe the best goal a man can have—a work of love.

—R. W. Loveless

Lawndale, Calif.
February 1973

chapter 1

the modern knife

Interest in benchmade knives is spreading like wildfire, fanned by the enthusiasm of collectors and hunters alike who are eager for information not only about fine knives, but about the men who craft them as well. This spectacular growth of interest in handmade and custom knives in recent years has been explained in many different ways, and perhaps, in truth, there is more than one valid explanation for it.

Bob Loveless, one of the most thoughtful of modern knifemakers, explains it quite simply: "We're so surrounded by mediocrity in our daily lives that there is a rising hunger for quality in our country. The custom knifemaker charges enough for a knife to be able to make a fine one, and thus he pleases both himself and his customer."

The fact that grown men will cheerfully part with two weeks' salary for a handmade hunting knife should come as no surprise to anyone who is familiar with American history, however. For despite our country's leadership in mass production, there is a very old and deeply rooted tradition of hand craftsmanship in America's past. From the time the Pilgrims landed until the industrial revolution in the mid-1800s, most of what was required was crafted singly and by hand. But in the past century, as mass production has become more and more the standard method of manufacturing, the phrase "handmade" has increasingly come to connote quality and desirability.

In spite of the seemingly sudden hurrah for the handmade knife, the making of fine cutlery is something that never actually died in our country, as we shall see; it simply lay dormant, kept alive by a handful of master cutlers, until it began to gain new life as scores of talented and imaginative men were drawn to the forge and grinding wheel during the last decade. Ten years ago there were hardly more than a dozen such cutlers in the land, but today there are at least a hundred, and the boom continues.

The knife as such has played a very special role in American history. Indeed, it is fair to say that if the history of Europe was carved with the sword, then the history of the United States was carved with a knife. Whatever the early American was, whether trapper, explorer, buffalo hunter, settler, trader or soldier, the chances are that he carried a knife. He probably had a gun—a Kentucky rifle, a Hawken, a Sharps, a Colt or a Winchester—but he certainly had a knife and always carried it on him.

One of our most spectacular bits of folklore is built around a particular knife and its originator's skill in using it—the Bowie knife. Most people have heard of Jim Bowie, but do not realize that he represented the pinnacle of a bloody and widespread tradition on the American frontier—that when the argument grew serious enough, it was settled with cold steel. Before the perfection of the revolver, the knife was *the* preferred sidearm, and the number of duels it figured in is quite astonishing.

In Bowie's day, a well-made knife was literally worth your life, and the smith who could turn out fine work commanded very fancy prices. From this you can see that we are not so much witnessing the birth of a new tradition, today, as the resurgence of an old one. For the modern knifemaker, like the fine custom gunsmith or engraver, is helping to restore the art of knifemaking to its historical level of excellence—and sometimes even beyond it.

But why all the fuss? Doesn't a store-bought knife work just as well? A fair question, for some commercial manufacturers do commendable work and their blades will satisfy many customers. Even the strongest supporter of handmade knives would have to admit that outfits like Buck, Gerber, Schrade-Walden, and Western Cutlery turn out excellent cutlery at very reasonable prices. Interestingly enough, however, the trend even with these companies has been toward higher quality and price until some of their premium blades now compare with and overlap the lower range of handmade knives.

If you are really critical in comparing the difference between a factory knife and one handmade by a skilled craftsman, you will not mistake the better product. However, the price, too, will be higher.

In addition, the personal factor is important. The handmade knife buyer invariably becomes interested in the man who builds his knife. The knife-maker's opinion on steels, his thoughts on design and his philosophy about his work all have interest and value for the paying customer, because of the close sense of identity between the man and his work. Conversely, serious knifemen want to know something about their clients, too. In a business where much of the selling is done on the telephone, a complete understanding is a prime requisite for a successful operation and happy customers.

Later on we'll visit with some knifemakers and find out from them what their business is really all about. But first, let's clarify our frame of reference a bit, beginning with some of the cutler's terminology. In recent years many terms have been so carelessly used that they have become almost mean-ingless. However, we'll try to give you an understanding of the basic language you'll read on the pages that follow.

A knife has two main parts, the handle and the blade. The blade's cutting or sharpened portion is called the edge. The top of the blade is termed the back, or spine, and if it has a curve, no matter how slight, that's known as the sweep. The various planes and angles ground into the blade are bevels, and if done well, they add great beauty to the lines of the entire blade.

The back of the blade, that is, the part running from the point to the spine, is called the false edge, and if sharpened, it is called the swedge. If the back is sharpened full-length, as with fighting knives, the knife is called a double-edged knife. Another blade detail, although one rarely seen on handmade knives, is a groove along the side of the blade. This is the fuller, commonly called the blood groove though it was originally forged into the blade for strength.

On many knives, but not all, you'll find a slight inward curve on the sharpened edge of the blade near the handle. This is called the choil, or in modern terminology, the finger cutout or finger clip. Its purpose, particularly on knives without guards, is to prevent your fingers from slipping down onto the sharpened blade. The experienced knife user may place a first or second finger in the choil for finer control when skinning game. In fact, you may even find choils on the handle itself. The ricasso is that portion of the blade right in front of the guard, but if there is a choil or finger clip that remains unsharpened in that spot just forget it.

Next in line is the guard or hilt. The small crossbars extending from each side of the hilt are the quillions. These may be double or single. Complicated? Not really, because if you want to be fancy or a bit old-fashioned, you may refer to the whole guard as the quillion. While most sporting knives usually have a single guard, fighting blades should always have a double guard to protect your hand in combat and catch your opponent's blade.

What you enclose your hand about is the handle or grip. If a knife has a handle that completely encloses the tang, it's referred to as a narrow-tang knife, and not infrequently, a stick-handle knife. If the tang is exposed and follows the general width of the blade it's a full-tang knife, and the various materials covering the sides are known as scales or slabs.

Should your knife be extra fancy it may have a small gold or silver inlay on one side of the handle. This is the escutcheon plate and is used for name or initials. Coming down the grip to the very end or top is the butt or pommel. It may be brass or nickel silver. In some cases there may be no actual butt at all, but this part of the knife is called the pommel.

This is the language of knives. It may sound confusing at first, but it is simple to master and it will add to your pleasure, too, for talking about fine knives is part of the fun.

In much that has been written about knives of late there is a confusion between "custom" and "handmade" knives, these terms being often used interchangeably. However, there is a big difference. Andy Russell makes the distinction very simply: "All custom knives are handmade, but not all handmade knives are custom." A custom knife is exactly that—a knife crafted to the customer's design, with the buyer usually supplying a rough sketch or even a scale drawing indicating the precise measurements of blade shape and handle. He will also usually specify the type of steel to be used, the handle

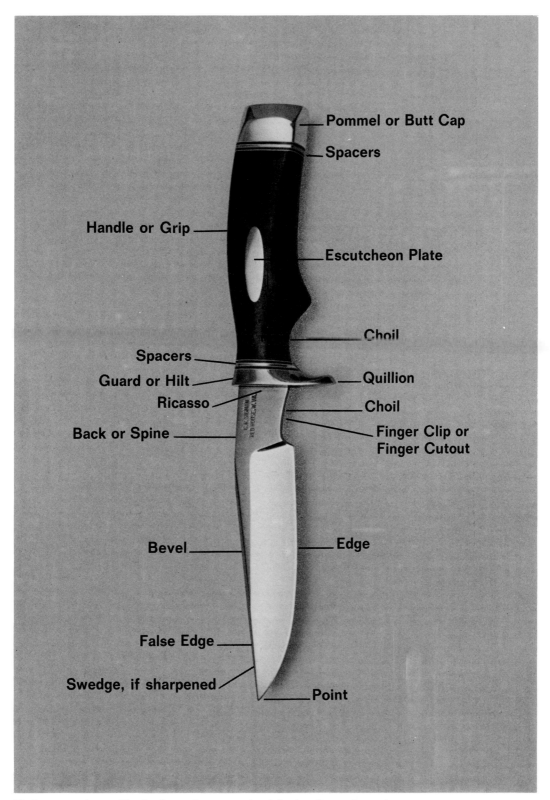

Pommel or Butt Cap

Spacers

Handle or Grip

Escutcheon Plate

Choil

Spacers

Guard or Hilt

Quillion

Ricasso

Choil

Back or Spine

Finger Clip or
Finger Cutout

Bevel

Edge

False Edge

Swedge, if sharpened

Point

Knife nomenclature. The knife is a fine example of Corbet Sigman's work.

material, the guard material (nickel silver or brass) and, frequently, the engraving on the blade or inlays on the grip. The knife thus ordered may take anywhere from six months to three years or longer to complete. What should such an *objet d'art* cost? The price could run into hundreds or even thousands of dollars, depending on the maker.

In contrast, a handmade knife, though not a production item in the ordinary sense, can usually be ordered from the maker's catalog that displays his regular line. Of course, most knifemakers offer enough options in the way of exotic woods, ivory, ebony and various bits of decoration to give you a tremendous choice in putting together exactly what you want in a knife. It may not be a custom knife in the full sense of the word, but you'll probably never find another like it around the same campfire.

That brings us to the next question usually asked by the novice: Are custom knives really *hand*made or do cutlers use machines and power tools? Of course they use machinery, since it would be pretty difficult to work steels and other hard materials with your bare hands. But the hands must come into it. Corbet Sigman, a prolific talker on the subject of craftsmanship, puts it this way: "A knife is handmade as long as the knife or tool, or both knife and tool, are hand-held during all shaping and finishing operations. If a knife is put into a jig for any grinding or milling it can no longer be called handmade."

In essence, a benchmade knife embodies the heart and creative skills of one man, who has devoted many long hours in cutting, grinding and polishing to bring forth a blade as fine as his talents will allow. Rod "Caribou" Chappel, a true creative artist in wood and steel, once said, "When a man buys a handmade knife he is also buying something of the immortality of the maker." There are, of course, degrees of immortality, and not every man who calls himself a knifemaker is a master craftsman. The old saw about all men being created equal, but some more equal than others, holds true for knifemaking. There are craftsmen who are real artists and build knives with a skill that delights the eye. Many others are first-rate, still growing in their ability, but basically delivering honest knives for honest dollars. And sadly, there are a few real hacks who will eventually drift out of the craft because their craftsmanship is indifferent or their relations with customers are poor.

For the money charged, then, how good a value really are the knives being offered today? In practical terms, it probably isn't possible to justify spending a couple of hundred bucks for a handmade knife. But for that matter, if sportsmen measured the cost of their toys in terms of pure utility, they'd never shoot another fine double or cast another split-cane flyrod. A fine knife, like a gun or a rod, is a highly personal object for a sportsman, and few things in this mass-production, machine-oriented world pay richer dividends in pride and satisfaction.

Few knifemakers would think of arguing that the optional extras on a knife make it cut any better; they just make it look prettier, hanging on your belt, which is, of course, a positive value, too. Actually, many knifemakers will try to talk you out of adding a lot of extras to their work, saying that things like ivory handles and nickel-silver guards simply add to the cost without adding anything functional. Listen to Bob Loveless, for example: "Most of this optional work, for which I must charge extra, is a waste of money. The best way to buy a Loveless knife is with linen Micarta handle slabs, and that's included in the basic price."

This may appear to be Loveless' honesty working overtime, but that's the way he is—direct and forthright, one of the poorest word-mincers I know. Take his guarantee (one of the best in the business, by the way): "I can make no promises about how well any of these knives will hold up for you, because I don't know how you'll use it, or how you'll take care of it. BUT, after getting your knife and working with it, on at least one hunt, and after putting it to the hone and getting to know it, IF then you don't feel it's worth what you paid me for it, THEN RETURN IT FOR A FULL AND PROMPT REFUND. There is no time limit, whether you take a month or a year." Bob does add a word of caution for the customer's guidance, adding, "If you return a knife to me that has been obviously abused, you'll find me asking some critical questions. . . . I've been in business for many years, and we both know what constitutes proper use of a hunting knife. Don't throw it, don't use it as an axe or pry-bar, and keep it clean and sharp, and you and I both will remember our dealings with pleasure."

Where did modern American knifemaking start? Any definite answer would be somewhat arbitrary, but you can make a pretty good case for saying that it started with a Michigan woodsman named William Scagel. It was Scagel who really inspired Randall, Randall who inspired Loveless, and from there on, the field grew too fast to keep track.

Bill Scagel died in 1963, but during the better part of his ninety years he enjoyed a reputation for fine knives that brought sportsmen tramping through the Michigan woods to his cabin door. Until Scagel decided to make knives—it was around 1920 that he began full-time—thoughts on blade shapes were pretty crude; a scaled-down Bowie was the most popular style. Bill Scagel decided there should be a number of specialized blade shapes, each capable of doing one job superbly, rather than one shape that did most jobs poorly. Although the big-bladed Bowies had some practical use, their size made them impractical for cleaning small game, filleting fish and skinning larger animals. Each Scagel knife was crafted for a particular purpose, many being short-bladed, with a flat back, allowing exquisite control in skinning and caping. Scagel often dispensed with a guard, but the grips were curved to fit the hand, and the result was a blade that was practically an extension of the finger. Scagel had an eye for the unusual, and anaconda ribs, hippo teeth and elephant ivory adorned his handles.

In later years, Scagel became something of a recluse, living in an isolated cabin with his dogs as his only companions. Some long-forgotten argument with the local power company left him without electricity, and he ingeniously devised an intricate system of pulleys and belts to drive his machinery from an ancient gas engine. He also made his own sanding discs, buffing wheels and the other paraphernalia a cutler needs to make a knife.

The crafting of fine hunting knives was Bill Scagel's passion, and he followed his profession until the last few years of his life, when crippling arthritis in both hands ended his work forever. Scagel knives weren't cheap, even in the 1930s; his regular knives brought $8 or $10, his fancy work $40 or $50. But they were a good investment: today, if you're lucky enough to find a

7

Knives of the early makers. The first three (left to right) are by the great master William Scagel. The next one is by Rudy Ruana, and the remaining two are early efforts of the late Harry Morseth.

genuine Scagel (a small curved dagger on the blade was his hallmark), you might pay $300 for the privilege of adding it to your collection.

The man who more than any other started the present knife craze is Walter Doane "Bo" Randall, Jr., of Orlando, Florida. A graduate of Ohio State, Randall didn't start out to be a knifemaker, nor did he even have the basic skills of many fledgling craftsmen. Bo Randall started out by managing his family's Florida orange groves and the Champion Paper Mill Company of Ohio, also largely owned by his family. However, he used all his available spare time to pursue his hobbies of hunting and fishing. In 1937, when he was twenty-seven, Randall happened to notice an unusually fine knife that was being used to scrape the bottom of an old boat. On closer examination it turned out to be a Scagel, and the die was cast. Randall, who had a craftsman's eye even at this stage, liked the knife so well he decided to copy it. His early efforts were so successful that before long he could not make enough knives to fill his orders.

The Randall reputation has been maintained for thirty-six years, and Randall's insistence on quality has never faltered, although his business has now grown to such size that he rarely has time to craft knives himself any more. Almost thirty different models are displayed in his present catalog, with enough combinations of blade length, handle materials and other options to make your selection almost unlimited.

Although Randall refuses to accept the blame for starting any wars, his handmade fighting knives have probably seen more action than those of all the other makers combined. The Project Mercury astronauts carried Randall knives into space on their epochal flight. (Their special model may still be ordered as No. 17.) U-2 pilot Francis Gary Powers had a Randall Trout & Bird knife along when he was shot down over Russia, and a Randall Raymond Thorpe Bowie and Arkansas toothpick were ordered for the late King Faisal II of Iraq.

Today, many Randall knives are in the collections of famous museums. The Museum of Modern Art in New York displays the Pro-Thrower as an example of fine design. The Camp & Trail model reposes in the Harvard Museum, and a Randall Bowie and a Diver's knife are displayed at the Smithsonian Institution in Washington, D.C.—fine tributes to a man who decided the world needed a better knife half a lifetime ago.

As we have said, Bob Loveless considers Randall responsible for his being in the knife business. Many years ago Loveless walked into New York's Abercrombie & Fitch and tried to buy a Randall knife. Told he'd have to wait at least nine months, Bob walked out and vowed he'd make his own. The next time he visited the store, the cutlery buyer gave him an immediate order. Those were the famous Delaware Maid blades, and if Bob had to wait nine months for a Randall, now his own customers have to wait twice that long for a Loveless, so the process has come full circle.

Loveless refuses to make anything except working knives and has no truck with Bowies, push daggers or what he calls "wall hangers." Anyone asking for them gets short shrift from the Loveless shop. With his business constantly growing, Bob found it impossible to maintain production and fulfill delivery schedules with any accuracy. In early 1971 he took on a young man, Steve Johnson, as a full-time partner. Steve had served his apprenticeship with Gil Hibben, Harvey Draper and Rod Chappel.

Actually, so much praise has been lavished on Loveless knives these past few years that even Bob laughingly admits, "There are several things even a Loveless knife won't do, like cure the common cold or help a hunter's marital problems."

Where have the rest of the current crop of knifemakers come from? There's no single answer, for hardly any two started off in the same way. Some were skilled hobbyists who made knives the way other people make ship models, and found they could get paid for it. Others were consciously looking for a vocation that offered wide scope for hand craftsmanship and individual creativity. Some got into knifemaking after retiring from other careers, like George Stone, who had been a metallurgist and knew his steels. Others were forced to give up their careers when the avocational aspect of their knifemaking gradually faded out.

Give or take a few, there are still only a couple dozen full-time professional knifemakers in the trade. The rest build knives part-time, though sometimes the dividing line is very slim. For example, Frank Centofante of Tampa, Florida, is a lieutenant in his city's fire rescue service, but also considers himself a full-time knifemaker since he puts in well over forty hours a week crafting very superior knives.

The fact that a maker is basically a part-time knifemaker in no way detracts from his ability, for some of the very best are part-timers. For example, Ted Dowell is an assistant professor of mathematics at Central Oregon Community College; Pete Heath is a radio dispatcher with the Sheriff's Department in Winnecone, Wisconsin; and John Owens is a Miami-based pilot for Pan Am. Even a first-class knifemaker like Chubby Hueske runs a seismograph outfit when he isn't grinding blades. Hueske crafts magnificent knives, and some of his latest efforts, new full-tang models with hollow-ground blades and finely tapering tangs, keep him in the top ranks of today's knifemakers.

Wanting to find out just what it takes to make a knifemaker, I asked Jess Horn, a part-time knifemaker and full-time engineer with the California Department of Highways, and he summed it all up this way: "A knifemaker is a determined craftsman with unending problems, but whose problems help him learn, so that his next knife will be a little better. He is always seeking new ways to do a better job; he is constantly experimenting with methods and materials which often end with untold hours of lost time. A knifemaker is far more critical of his work than are most customers. He knows all the flaws in his work and tries to eliminate them. He is sensitive to comments on his knives, but when he receives a compliment it seems to make all the work worthwhile."

The list could go on—art instructor Bernard Sparks in the little town of Dingle, Idaho; marine biology teacher Don Zaccagnino of Pahokee, Florida; and so on. In spite of their varied backgrounds all these men have one thing in common: a love of knives and an artisan's skill in shaping raw materials into fine cutlery.

Not unlike actors, some knifemakers have reached star status through one memorable performance. Jess Horn is a prime example. Although he made excellent sheath knives for a number of years, he remained relatively unknown until he decided to build, of all things, a handcrafted replica of the old Remington Bullet Knife, a small, inexpensive folding knife manufactured by Remington Arms before the Second World War. When displayed at a knife show a few years ago, it proved an instant success. Even competitors laid down hard cash to obtain this beautifully made knife. The same thing happened to Ron Lake, another maker new to the game. Again, a folder shot this newcomer into prominence. Ron had decided there should be a folding knife strong enough to be used by a hunter yet compact enough to be carried in the pocket. His expertise with precision machinery (he's a tool and die maker) came in handy. The Lake knife was machined from a solid piece of brass and had a very neat way of releasing the locked blade. Ron toted the first model to the Houston Show in August of 1971 and took so many orders he's still running to catch up.

Despite the demand for benchmade knives, and the constant entry of new men into the field, no knifemaker can expect to become wealthy grinding blades. One man working alone can turn out only so many knives a year. Warren Page, in an article in *Field & Stream* a few years ago, calculated that a top knifemaker probably earns less than a union truck driver. I asked a number of makers about this, and they generally agreed. Jimmy Lile said that knifemaking was simply a way to get out of the rat race and still earn a reasonable living. Bob Loveless insists on earning a living in his shop and declares that he does so, but when pressed, he admits he made more money in a previous job. Dan Dennehy said there are usually two reasons why most people make knives: a plausible reason, and the real reason. Dan's plausible reason is that he wanted a particular style of knife and couldn't find it in the stores, so he accepted the challenge and made it himself. However, the real reason he gives is, "I was always fascinated by the Bowie story and Tarzan tales as a youngster. My love of adventure, wildlife and all the activity of the out-of-doors was always associated with knives, so when I got out of the Navy I went into knifemaking."

Obviously money, or the acquisition of wealth, is not the primary object of life for most of these men. For them, luxury is the freedom to do exactly what they want. Most knifemakers would be unhappy in any other endeavor. They are having a love affair with gleaming steel, and for a knife nut, that isn't hard to understand. More important, they are doing the one thing they do best, carrying on the tradition of fine craftsmen in cutlery.

Knifemakers as a group are so dedicated to their work that it is not uncommon for them to register considerable advances in artistic development and standards of craftsmanship in a surprisingly short period of time. A good example is Dwight Towell of Midvale, Idaho. Dwight works on knives only part-time, as do many craftsmen, and is relatively little known. However, after making knives for less than three years his work is already impeccable, with fine silver soldering and fit of blade to handle and guard (a weak point, incidentally, of many new knifesmiths). At present Dwight offers about ten models and his work is obviously influenced by Ted Dowell, but all his blades are hollow ground and buffed to a high mirror finish. The execution of his handles is also flawless, especially his singed curly maple and fine walnut burl. Towell's steel is a high-carbon tool steel that tests out to Rockwell 61. He will also craft blades of 440-C stainless if requested, and is happy to make you a custom knife if you don't care for his regular line.

There are several excellent knifemakers who seem to have received far less than their fair share of renown. Corbet Sigman told me that among the top men today you must mention Rod "Caribou" Chappel, Bob Dozier and Lloyd Hale (Sigman was obviously too modest to include himself). Alaska-born and of Indian heritage, Rod was sent to New York as a youngster, where he won, and first rejected, two college scholarships. (He was having too much fun as a professional Indian dancer.) Finally, however, he became a graduate engineer in industrial design, good enough to do many of the complicated drawings of the Atlas and Silo missile systems, as well as the Mercury Capsule.

Chappel got into the knife business when he ran into Gil Hibben and traded knives for know-how—what Rod designed Hibben built. Later, meeting Harvey Draper, he was asked to join him in the knife business, but preferring to live in Washington State, he declined. Draper told him if he felt that strongly about knifemaking, he should come down to Utah and he'd show Rod everything he knew. Moving in with Steve Johnson (now Loveless' partner), the men talked, lived and thought about knives fifteen hours a day for two weeks. Even now Rod remembers the burnt fingers, cuts and sore hands he got trying to build up the calluses of a knifemaker. Whatever success he's attained, Rod feels he owes it to Hibben and Draper. There are some critics who consider

Chappel's designs pretty far out, but Rod explains, "The design of a knife represents the sum of a man, his heritage and what he is." You have to hold a Chappel knife, and feel the balance of its flowing line to understand what one man is saying about design. His blades run the gamut from Gurkha kukris to a huge selection of Bowies, hunters and skinners. Reflecting his locale, the knives have names that point to the Pacific Northwest: Polar Cub, Cascade, Graywolf and Chief Joseph.

Lloyd Hale, now of Arkansas, was resident knifesmith for a couple of years at Black's Forge in Washington, Arkansas, where the original Bowie was supposedly made. Working at a replica of Black's Forge, Hale naturally crafted Bowies. Before getting into knifemaking full-time, he was a jack-of-all-trades, even making a guitar that he once sold for a handsome fee. The first knife Hale ever made was a Bowie. A friend asked if he would build a knife if the drawings were supplied. When his buddy began unfolding reams of paper, Hale admits he quaked in his boots, because as the roll was unwound he could see it was a Bowie. "The damn thing was tremendous and scared hell out of me," says Hale, "but I went after it and I'll admit building it wasn't as easy as I thought, but it wasn't as difficult either."

When the job was completed his friend was happy. Hale was delighted and decided right there his vocation was knifemaking. Now, since going on his own and leaving the security of Black's Forge, Hale has a few doubts about his success. It's the same fear everyone has of being on his own, but in the handful of years he's been crafting fine knives his climb has been steadily upward, and he has built a reputation for quality work. He must be included among the finest knifemakers in the country.

The first handmade knife Bob Dozier ever saw was made by George Stone, and the work impressed him mightily, so much so that he decided to try his hand at making a knife. Originally, Bob had been a structural-iron worker in Louisiana, and was probably influenced by his grandfather, a country blacksmith, who made knives on the side. When Bob started he built his own grinder and other equipment and often had to shut down his shop and go to work to earn a living. "Knifemakers aren't born," Bob told me. "It takes thousands of hours of frustration and disappointment, and there are times you just want to give it all up. The man who is taught to make knives in someone else's shop may not experience this, but the person who starts alone will know what I mean."

Dozier, a former resident of Springdale, in the small Arkansas belt that seems to attract so many fine knifemakers, prefers to make true custom knives to the client's order, rather than have a wide range of models shown in his catalog. Dozier strives to make a perfect knife, and admits to being his own hardest critic. Other knifemakers have called Bob a nitpicker regarding his own work, and Dozier says this is true but adds, "You must condition yourself to be critical. Otherwise you tend to accept the bad and never improve." A good knifemaker must be a combination of designer and craftsman, and Bob feels a beautiful knife without practical value has no reason for being. Dozier works very hard indeed to attain perfection, and feels a customer should expect to receive exactly what the maker promises.

Unlike many designers, Dozier never puts an idea to paper, likening his creative thoughts to a motion picture that runs continually through his mind while he's making a knife. "First you see the knife in your mind, then you begin," Dozier said.

Another craftsman with the same compulsion for perfection is Don Zaccagnino of Pahokee, Florida. A transplanted New Englander, Don is a marine biology teacher in the local high school, and his greatest production is during the summer school holiday. Zack (that name is his trademark) is a fine painter and sculptor and his knives can be considered art—they are an expression of his talents in wood and steel. While Zack's knives are still relatively unknown, they reach a perfection seldom seen in today's market. Zaccagnino's work may be instantly recognized by his use of a contoured butt and slanted guard, plus the distinctive shape of his blades.

What of really new makers like Gerry Jean of Manchester, Connecticut, or Lou Booth of Boonton, New Jersey, who brought knifemaking into the barren land of the eastern seaboard? (Until now most knifesmiths seem to have sprung from the South and West.) Jean's knives show great promise, and his most exciting designs are integral-hilt-and-butt knives selling for about half what better known makers charge. No doubt his prices will rise as success comes along, but for the present, his knives are considered bargains. Incidentally, he's one of the few makers I know who use oak for handles, probably because of his New England upbringing.

Lou Booth could be called a new maker, although he crafted his first knives some seventeen years ago in New Mexico. In and out of knifemaking for many years, he decided to go full-time last year. Booth has some interesting innovations, particularly a boot knife with a spring clasp attached to the handle. This enables the wearer to tuck it into a boot, belt or wristwatch strap sans sheath. Two other fascinating models are all-steel self-handled knives with blades less than three inches in length, one a skinner and the other for general utility.

Booth finds that crafting knives in the East calls for different blade styles. "In New Mexico everyone wanted large blades, often seven to nine inches, but here hunters want smaller knives, and the men who come to my shop seldom pick anything over four inches." Booth's handles are made of such exotic woods as bubinga or zebrawood, cross-cut for grain effect. Booth has a secret process (he refuses to discuss it) of treating the wood so that it brings out the texture and gives unusual beauty to the grip.

Along about now you've probably met enough knifemakers to understand something of what makes them tick and the kind of creativity they share. So now let's take a closer look at what they work with, the other main ingredient of the knife—steel.

chapter 2

steel, the heart of the knife

Steel is the heart of a knife, and any knifemaker can argue about what makes the finest knife steel. Indeed, they spend so much time experimenting and trying new alloys, you'd think they were trying to make gold from bats' wings and lead, like the ancient alchemists.

Certainly no one can fault them in this search for perfection, but the longer they argue over the merits of different steels, the more confusing it becomes. It should be accepted that any competent cutler will use the finest steels available, and what you are offered is that one knifemaker's concept of what will give you the finest cutting edge possible. If these craftsmen differ, as they frequently do and with great vehemence, that's as it should be. Bob Loveless, an experienced metallurgist, once walked into the research laboratory of one of our largest steel producers and asked which of their steels would make the best knife blade. Three highly skilled research metallurgists gave three different answers. So it is no wonder that each knifemaker has his own idea of the best steel for his particular knives.

The elusive "perfect steel" that knifemakers have sought over the centuries would have three principal qualities—it would never rust, never break and never have to be resharpened. Unfortunately, such a steel doesn't exist, never did and never will. What modern knifemakers do is to avail themselves of the best combination of these qualities they can obtain through dint of hard work, research, experimentation and the help of many top steel companies.

When you take the time to peruse the catalogs of various makers (and they make fascinating reading over a long winter's night) you'll discover that each offers slightly different steels, some even three or four. They provide slightly

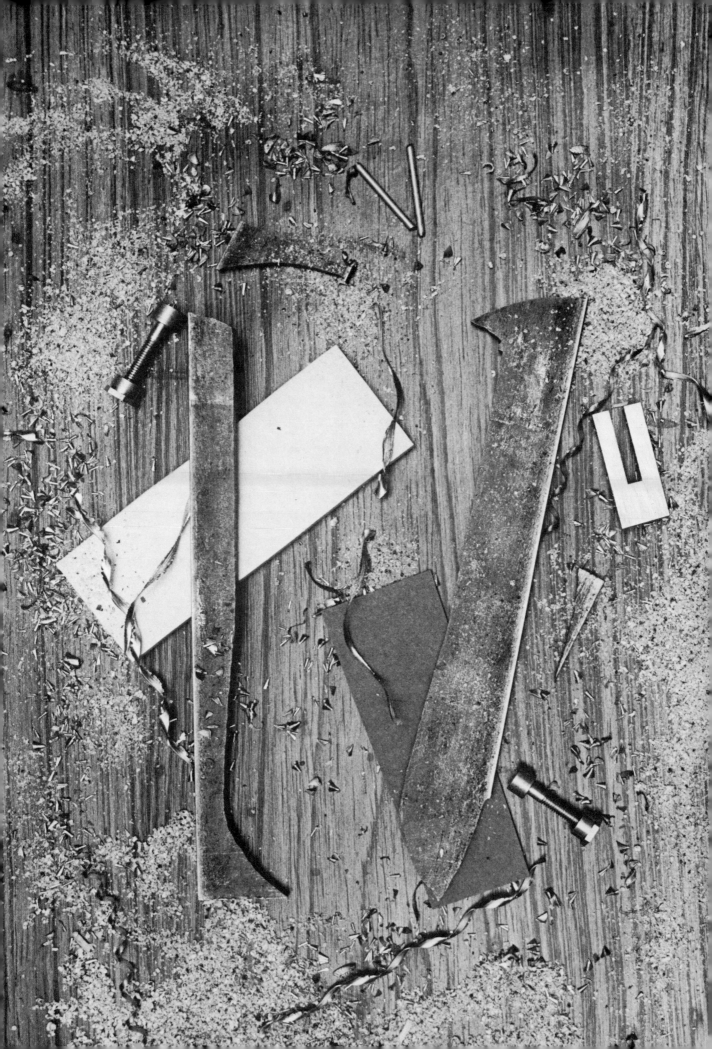

different ratios of these three qualities, and as a practical matter, any of them will make a finer blade than you've ever owned before. It's a simple fact that no knifemaker knowingly uses an inferior steel; the competition is too keen. Still, the best steel in the world won't make a decent blade unless it's properly ground and correctly heat-treated, and the finest heat-treat won't do a thing for inferior steel. You must have a combination of three things: fine steel, excellent grind and careful heat-treat to make a superior hunting knife.

What the cutler hopes to deliver, of course, is a well-balanced alloy of various elements in a steel that combines hardness and toughness, with an ability to resist corrosion reasonably well, and superior edge-holding ability. A problem arises, however, because you can't have everything at once, and that's where the hair-splitting of knifemaking comes in. Hardness isn't everything, and some makers, like Bo Randall, even prefer a softer steel because the blade is easier to sharpen. Others feel that blade sharpening isn't all that difficult, and that most hunters prefer a blade that holds an edge slightly longer without requiring sharpening.

One point of confusion is the fact that hardness and edgeholding are not precisely related, so let us digress for a moment. Throughout this chapter you'll note references to the "Rockwell scale." This is a fairly simple method of determining the relative hardness of steels which involves forcing a diamond point into a bar of steel or finished blade. The depth of the indent is measured and this gives the hardness. The problem is that the Rockwell readings tossed about by various makers don't mean much; they only prove that a particular piece of steel thus tested does have a certain hardness, and that's all. For example, there are several different types of steels that will test out to RC-68 that simply will not hold an edge as well as steels of RC-60.

Most knifemakers work with tool steels having a carbon content of about 1 percent, or 440-C stainless. However, when more tungsten and cobalt are added, steel leaves the range of tool steel and enters the realm of high-speed steel, which has quite different properties.* The tungsten, cobalt, and other additions make some of these steels almost too hard for knife blades, and they can become fairly brittle in use. Most of these steels are used for cutting other steels, and they are sometimes called "red-hot" steels because they actually turn cherry-red when being used, while retaining their ability to do their job. Blades this hard are much more difficult to sharpen, and when steels move into very high Rockwell ratings, 67 or 68, in the opinion of many experts they have passed the bounds of reason. They do indeed hold an edge under extreme use, but often they have to be returned to the maker for resharpening, and this just isn't practical. Sure, there are customers for this type of steel, just as there are always a couple of fellows around who want something special, and some knifemakers do offer a few of these unusual grades. In practice, though, they are really a bother.

Most customers willingly accept the word of a master knifesmith regarding the steel to be used. Many cutlers won't even discuss the ingredients of their steels, and this is valid. After all, they did the research and experiments, and are entitled to a couple of secrets. But any maker who has been crafting blades

* Tables showing the composition of the eight most popular knife steels appear on page 33.

longer than two or three years should be expected to use a wisely chosen steel and should be relied upon to provide a dependable knife.

Ted Dowell, a fine knifemaker from Bend, Oregon, has said about steels: "The life of a knifemaker would be simple indeed were there a single steel available which would offer all the desirable properties that a best-quality knife should have, and offer them in large measure. The maker of benchmade knives doesn't want a good blade, he wants the very best he can produce using the best that modern metallurgy can offer in the way of steel composition and heat treatment. If he knowingly settles for less, he is cheating himself as a craftsman and you as the customer."

The heat treatment of a knife is a never-ending problem for many knifemakers. Simply put, the finished blades are placed in a furnace, usually electronically controlled, brought to a predetermined temperature for a certain length of time and then quenched in oil, brine or air. Because of the cost of a furnace, many craftsmen have their blades treated commercially, but others have actually built their own furnaces and learned the complicated art of heat-treating. But the search for a better steel and finer methods of heat treatment is never-ending for the serious knifemaker.

The qualities Dowell feels are important in a knife blade are toughness, abrasion resistance, hardness and, sometimes, corrosion resistance. The relative importance given to each by a particular knifemaker will determine the steel he uses. While we're on the subject of Dowell, let's take a look at the three steels he uses and the reasons. If a steel is tough, then its abrasion resistance is low, and vice versa. Ted solves this in part by offering three steels: one with high abrasion resistance, F-8; one very tough, D-2; and one stainless, 440-C. The F-8 steel will hold an edge better than any other, Dowell claims. Its Rockwell hardness is 60. D-2 is a new steel Dowell has been experimenting with and he may eventually replace the F-8 and settle on D-2 and 440-C. Ted's advice on blades is simply to select 440-C if you want a display piece or if you intend to expose your knife to rust-promoting conditions, and to select either F-8 or D-2 if edge-holding is of primary concern.

Bob Loveless is another maker who has delved into the intricate world of metallurgy in his search for the ultimate blade. In more than nineteen years of crafting fine knives, Loveless has used a dozen different tool steels and admits he has gotten fairly good working results from most. Yet it became apparent to Bob years ago that nobody in the field had spent much time and money researching the problem of the ideal knife steel. Bob said, "I learned to stop believing everything written in the steelmakers' catalogs, and started to study the subject myself."

Some seven years ago he looked for a steel company that would be interested enough in the problem to make up a special alloy to his order with low limits held on impurities and with special handling in melting and rolling. Such a company was eventually found in Pennsylvania, and, after several months, Loveless received his shipment of slightly less than seven hundred pounds of his very own steel. Bob used and discarded about fifty pounds of this expensive mixture just learning the tricks of heat-treating it, but found that the material did give what he'd been seeking all along: a very high toughness in terms of ultimate yield (the point at which steel will bend, but not break) and exceptional torsional impact strength (a measure of the blade edge's ability to resist damage when severely used) with a relatively high hardness, in excess of RC-61.

Loveless knife blades from this steel gave performance in the field never before possible with any standard tool steel, and customers were swift in voicing praise. It was a great steel, but Bob admits, "While it made knives that held a cutting edge extremely well, my honesty compels me to add that it also rusted well, too." After learning all he could from this steel during four years of use, Loveless laid out a further research program and ordered some six different tool steels, all slightly different in alloy content, and the results were once again checked with practical usage in the field. With all his research completed, it appears that Bob's search ended accidentally.

During a casual conversation with the West Coast manager of a New York steel company, Bob learned of a new steel developed for the high-temperature regions of the jet engines in the Boeing 747 aircraft. The material was alloyed to hold strength at 700 degrees, and Bob's examination of the alloy structure, plus a study of the manufacturer's heat-treating procedures, led him to believe it would make a superior knife steel. Loveless initially ordered five hundred pounds, which was delivered in August of 1971. He immediately made knives and placed them in the hands of hunting friends in the western part of the United States and Canada. It didn't take long for favorable reports to filter back, and within weeks, Bob was assured of the superior qualities of these blades. He realized this could be the steel he'd been seeking all these years. The blades didn't rust in normal use; even a knife made for a skindiver didn't pit after long immersion in salt water, and the material actually held up better than his old silico-manganese alloy.

What is amazing about these new knives is the fact that they are placed in service at the high Rockwell hardness of RC-61-62, yet are quite ductile. The most unusual characteristic of the steel is the secondary rehardening quality. Simply explained, the blade quenches after soaking at 2000°F., attaining a hardness of RC-58 at that time. Then, during the tempering operation, it picks up more hardness and strength as the Martensite transformation (a transfer from a coarse to a fine grain structure within the steel) completes itself. The significance of secondary rehardening is this: The maximum strength is achieved during tempering rather than first quench as in the usual grade of tool steel. The result is a complete lack of brittle structure, and the achievement of maximum strength. Those knife fanciers who have followed Bob's career over the years know of his insistence that the costly benchmade knife must far surpass any other knife or it has no sound justification.

Since the end of September 1971, Loveless has been using this new grade of 154-CM alloy steel in all his knives and expects to continue to use it. Bob's prime interest is what can be accomplished with steel. "At times people think my knives are rather thin, but we get very few back," Loveless said.

Corbet Sigman, like Loveless and Dowell, is a perfectionist who has dug into steel research with the persistence of a ferret. Before turning to knife-making full time, Sigman was a chemical technician who decided to stay home when his company relocated its plant. His research training, combined with impeccable skill as a knifemaker, gives him an edge on the subject of steels.

Sigman's credo on handcrafted knives is simple: "Superior edge-holding ability and careful workmanship are the only reasons for the existence of the custom knife market, and I place equal emphasis on both when crafting a knife." Sigman offers three steels to his clients and carefully explains what each will do and what should be expected. His top-rated steel is a carbon tool steel, type W-2, of the best available grade for hunting knives with a carbon content of 1.10 percent. Sigman feels that W-2, in terms of purity (lack of silica or sand in the mix), is one of the most highly developed steels and makes the best knife.

There are dozens of tool steels for the knifemaker to choose from, and most containing appreciable amounts of other metals (or elements) are called alloy tool steels. Some of these elements are tungsten, molybdenum, vanadium, chromium, cobalt, and silicon. Added to steel in varying amounts, they will give a definite characteristic to the steel such as heat, abrasion or shock resistance. In the opinion of the knifemaker the qualities he deems important, from his own experience, are what he offers his customers.

What Sigman wants in a blade are excellent edge-holding ability and ease of sharpening, both found in abundance in W-2. This steel, when quenched in cool brine, will have a hardness of RC-67-68, and after tempering will be brought down to RC-63-64. A high carbon-chrome content, plus high hardness, will make a blade that will retain a keen edge exceptionally well. Brine, incidentally, is a drastic quenching medium and great care must be taken in preparing blades for heat-treating. Blades must be ground as symmetrical as possible and polished to perfection; otherwise quenching will cause cracking or warpage because of uneven surface stresses. Sigman finds W-2 a temperamental steel and cannot craft a blade longer than six inches from it because of its distortion factor, but since most blades for field use will usually be shorter, this doesn't bother him too much. W-2 can also be oil-treated, and it will produce a good knife, but it will not be quite as hard and consequently will not hold an edge quite as long as the brine-treated variety.

Another steel used by Sigman, especially for blades over six inches, is O-1, an oil-hardening steel. This is a good tough steel, but its working hardness—RC 60-61—is not as high as that of type W-2. Sigman's third steel, and one offered by almost all knifemakers, is 440-C stainless. A much maligned steel in the past, it has now come to be accepted as an excellent knife steel due to its high chromium content and fairly high abrasion resistance. Admittedly, it will not hold an edge quite as well as some other steels, and has an inherent brittleness that cannot be entirely eliminated by heat-treating, but this is not to imply that fine knives cannot be crafted from 440-C. Edge brittleness or lack of strength in the cutting edge is the main problem, and if a 440-C blade is ground too thin or treated roughly you will see tiny nicks or chips on the edge under a strong glass. This problem can be eliminated in part by grinding the edge a bit thicker, although this sacrifices ease of cutting because of the greater resistance of a fatter edge. Sigman overcomes this by freezing the 440-C after quenching to −100° F. in order to gain more hardness. Sigman, like other makers, also recently began to use 154-CM.

The biggest objection to alloy steel by many knifemakers is its typically high abrasion resistance. Tool steels containing appreciable amounts of molybdenum or tungsten must be tempered back to a hardness of around RC-60, or even less, in order to have the necessary low abrasion resistance for a useful knife. Even at that hardness some of these steels are brittle, and having been brought down from the point where they excel, RC-64-66, much of their edge-holding ability is lost. While knives containing these elements are excellent in the edge-holding department, they are also very difficult to sharpen because of the presence of these excess carbides. In Sigman's opinion, chromium in anything over the trace amounts needed to control hardness is deleterious to the edge-holding of fine cutlery steel. It may appear contrary to the layman that abrasion resistance can be too much of a good thing when it would appear to be one of the factors contributing to a sturdy knife. Yet a knife can be too hard and too tough to be practical.

One point should be made about so-called stainless steel. It might be better if stainless steels were referred to as "rust-resistant" or "stain-resistant," for stain they will eventually. Any steel, particularly carbon steels, will discolor with use, but 440-C is less prone to this and retains its beauty for a longer time than most other steels.

One of the most interesting and unusual steels was introduced by the late Harry Morseth some forty years ago. Morseth, one of the early pioneers in crafting handmade blades, imported a Norwegian laminated steel consisting of a hard-tempered, high-carbon steel core forged between layers of soft, ductile iron. For centuries the toughest swords and knives had had these carefully forged composites of steel and iron, and Morseth, an American of Norwegian descent, was the first to bring this method to modern knifemaking. Morseth blades have a hardness of RC-63-64, and the novelty of this blade is that it can be placed in a vise and bent back and forth without breaking. Although this has been demonstrated at knife shows for years, neither the writer nor the maker recommend subjecting your Morseth knife to the test!

Not only do opinions differ over steels, there is also a controversy over forging versus stock removal. In fact, to even mention forging in some quarters will probably bring up another argument that never ceases among knifemakers: Since modern mills do such a fine job of forging, why forge again? Some makers answer that the mill's rollers impart a directional action to the grain structure of the steel under great pressure. If the knifemaker could take advantage of this while making a blade, well and good, except that the curve of the blade must, at one time or another, run against this grain structure.

Gil Hibben was one of the very early knifemakers to forge 440-C in the days when it came in rolls. When it became available in flat stock he ceased forging and went to the stock-removal method. Sigman forges only one steel, W-2, and the reason he doesn't forge the others is that the more complicated a steel becomes in alloy content the more important it is to have accurate temperature control during the forging operation. Sigman feels he cannot control the heat this closely when hammering a thin cross-section of metal. Since type W steels are reasonably simple carbon steels—if any steel could be called simple—they are consequently the easiest steel to forge. The basic reason Sigman forges the W-2 is that the forging action of the rolling mill imparts a directional characteristic to the bar. As long as the benefits derived from the mill are realized, and as long as the edge of the knife is parallel to the rolling

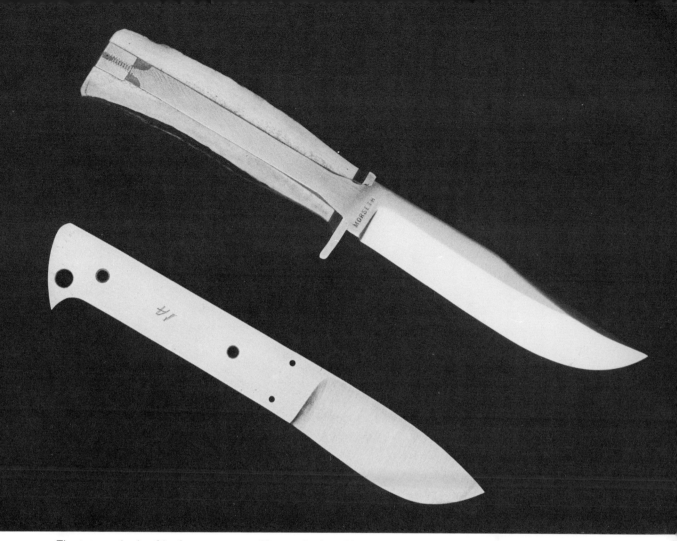

The two methods of knife construction. The top knife, a Morseth, shows the narrow-tang method. Note the wide section of metal left near the blade to prevent breaking or cracking. At the end of the tang is a threaded butt screw to take up all slack and achieve a secure fit. The hollow part of the handle is also filled with epoxy for added strength. The bottom blade is the beginning of a full-tang model by Bob Dozier. Handle slabs of various materials are fastened to each side, then ground and polished to shape.

direction of the bar from which the blade is cut, all is well. Unfortunately, when the curve of the blade has to be cut across this pattern, trouble arises. This is due to impurities such as silicon or sand being stretched in the direction in which the bar is rolled, and these leave tiny voids acting as notches in the metal. Sigman's frustration with steel is that of many skilled craftsmen. "You may be surprised to learn," he told me recently, "that steel contains so many impurities. But I have yet to see a single bar completely free from defects, and I buy the best I can get." For that reason Sigman reforges to break up the directional pattern established in rolling and sets a new and more favorable grain direction in the blades.

How much better is a forged blade than one shaped by stock removal? Not much, says Sigman. It depends quite a lot on the characteristic of the particular bar of steel from which the blade was cut. Forging and the subsequent anneal he gives his forged blade do tend to make everything uniform from one knife to another. The anneal, incidentally, is absolutely essential if benefits are to be derived from forging. Annealing is a slow cooling process from above the critical temperature, and requires several hours of carefully controlled temperatures to bring the steel down to normal. Annealing refines

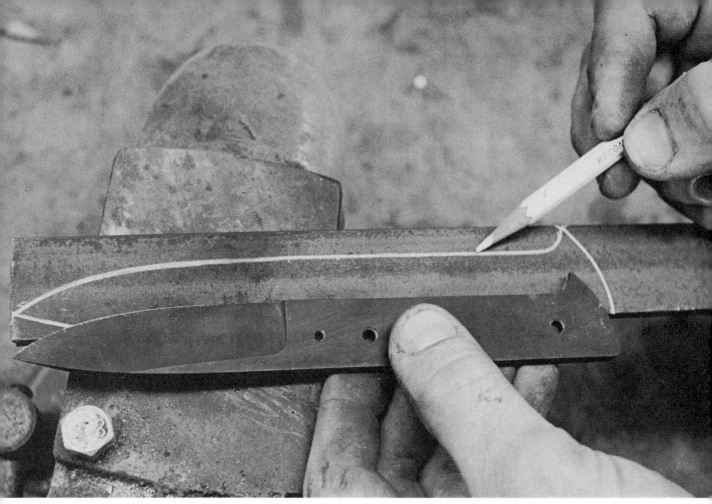

1 Bob Dozier takes us through the steps of crafting a full-tang knife. The first step is marking the outline of the blade on a piece of steel.

2 The outline is cut from the steel bar with a bandsaw.

3 Smoothing and shaping the rough blade on a belt grinder.

4 Shaping the blade. The blade cannot be allowed to become too hot and must be dipped in water frequently.

5 Drilling holes in the tang for the handle rivets.

6 The guard, in this case of nickel silver, is carefully filed to fit the blade.

7 Dozier solders the guard to the blade. The soldering requires skill; if it is not done properly, there will be pinholes and excess solder.

8 The guard is roughly shaped with a round file. The blade is protected from the vise jaws by a fiber sheath.

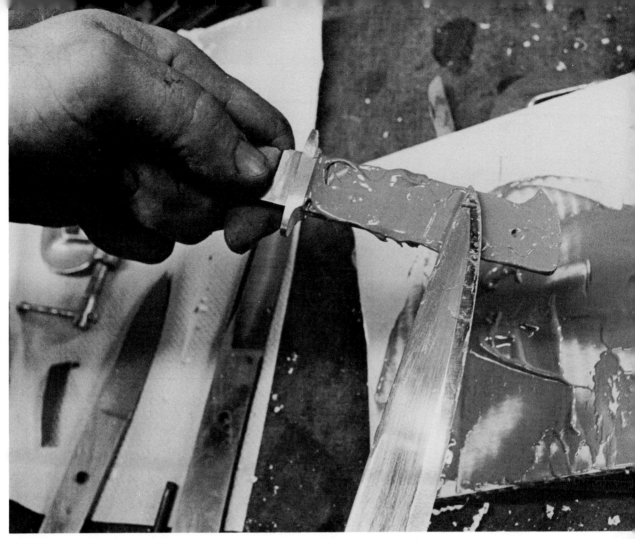

9 Industrial epoxy is generously smeared over the tang to hold the handle slabs.

the crystal structure of the blades and leaves them in the optimum condition for hardening.

Forging is a much more difficult method of making a knife than by stock removal. A forged blade must be ground to trueness, whereas a blade sawed from a bar is already true and the only thing necessary is to grind off unwanted steel from both sides of the bar. (But it is necessary to anneal blades shaped by stock removal because of stresses set up by the rough grind operation.) Since Corbet Sigman uses both techniques he honestly feels his opinion is unbiased. Forging, properly done with the anneal, is a lot of extra work with very little gain in quality, yet Sigman feels it's well worth the additional effort when crafting blades from carbon steel.

There is no doubt that forging in the hands of a man with the skills of Sigman or Bill Moran will make a beautiful knife, and some makers forge simply because they enjoy this method of crafting a blade. If they have the skills necessary they will make a flawless blade, but in the hands of amateurs, forging is dangerous because they forge more flaws than quality into the blade. Since forging is often regarded as a more difficult method of shaping a blade the majority of cutlers use the stock removal method, which means that the rough form of the blade is first sawed from a blank of steel and then ground and polished into shape. If you think that's easy, try making a knife from an old file some day.

A short time ago, wanting to learn as much as possible about knifemaking,

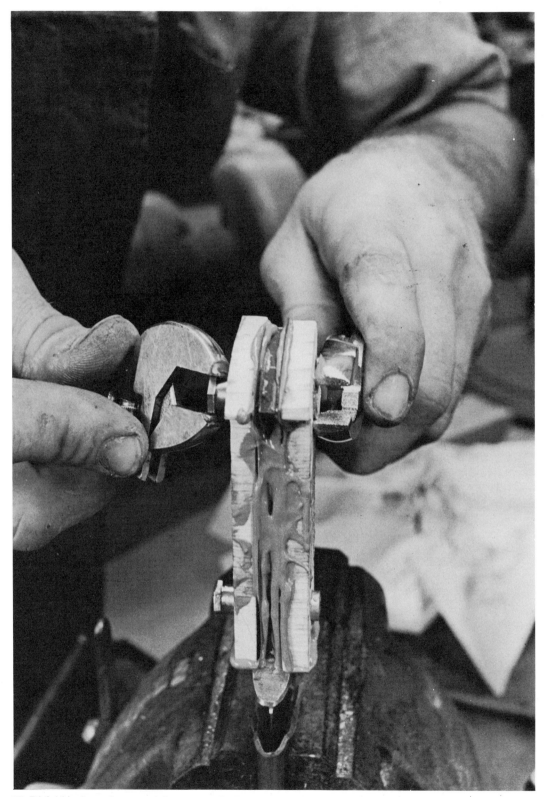

10 Roughly shaped ivory slabs are applied to tang. Note rivets being taken up to achieve proper thickness of epoxy layer.

I spent a couple of weeks in Arkansas visiting the shop of Andy Russell's Morseth knives and hanging over Bob Dozier's shoulder at his workbench. Both men, with infinite patience, took me through the steps of crafting a knife. I did all that was required of a budding knifemaker—I burned my fingers, cut a thumb, inhaled emery dust and admired my grind much too long before plunking the hot blade into a bucket of water. Consequently, I ended up with a knife that might be used as a prime example to illustrate the finer points of what a benchmade knife should not be. Burnt steel, uneven bevels, a marvelously undulating edge grind which I defy any knifemaker to emulate, and a choice selection of pinholes in the overabundance of silver solder where blade meets the guard. With pardonable pride my handle was excellent and received generous compliments, no doubt to assuage my feelings.

As they say of French wines, it was a good knife but not a great knife, and my ordeal by fire gave me a much greater respect for the skills of knifemaking. It isn't easy to grind bevels that meet on both sides, nor is it simple to grind an edge along a hot blade. Even fitting a handle requires some half-dozen different steps and each one can go wrong, completely ruining your previous efforts. The skills of polishing require exceptional care, and too much pressure against the polishing wheel can change the lines of a blade. In truth, I found the skills of a knifemaker to be very challenging and most knifesmiths will admit to making hundreds, sometimes thousands, of blades before they have secure command of the proper techniques. Frank Centofante goes

11 After epoxy has set overnight, rivets are filed flush and handle is shaped.

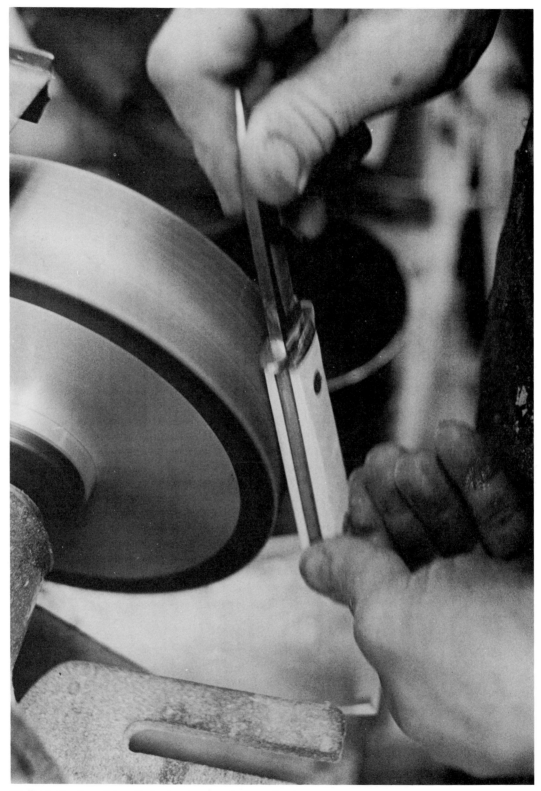

12 Final shaping of handle is done on a grinding wheel.

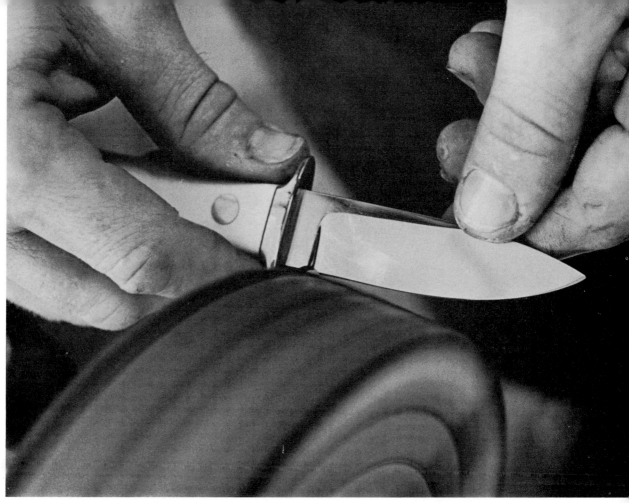

13 Final polishing of blade. Great care must be exercised at this point since the slightest error may cause bevels to vary from side to side.

14 A completed boot knife by Bob Dozier.

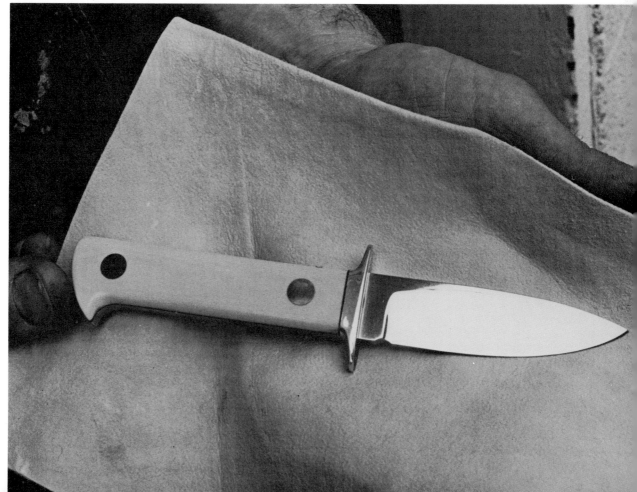

Clyde Fischer supplies kits of materials for knifemaking—the steel blade blank, brass hilt blank, and stag handle. Morseth Knives supplies complete kits with finished blade and guard attached.

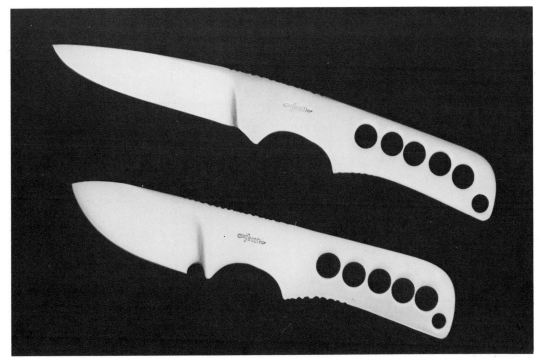

The modern concept in knifemaking—two samples of the latest self-handled knives of Lou Booth. Both are of 154-CM steel with circular handle cutouts for lightness.

Composition of the most popular knifemaker's steels

This list shows the percentage of each element in each steel. Iron, of course, accounts for at least 80 percent of these steels; only the elements added to the iron are listed here.

154-Cm	Carbon	1.05	W-2	Carbon	.06/1.4	
	Manganese	0.60		Manganese	.25	
	Phosphorus	0.030		Silicon	.25	
	Sulfur	0.030		Vanadium	.25	
	Silicon	0.25				
	Chromium	14.00	M-2	Carbon	.85	
	Molybdenum	4.00		Manganese	.25	
				Phosphorus	.00	.03 max.
440-C	Carbon	1.00		Sulfur	.00	.03 max.
	Manganese	.50		Silicon	.30	
	Silicon	.40		Chromium	4.20	
	Chromium	17.05		Molybdenum	5.00	
	Molybdenum	.45		Tungsten	6.35	
	Nickel	.20		Vanadium	1.90	
F-8	Carbon	1.30	A-2	Carbon	1.00	
	Tungsten	8.00		Manganese	.50/.70	
	Chromium	4.00		Silicon	.25/.40	
	Vanadium	.25		Chromium	5.00	
				Molybdenum	1.00	
D-2	Carbon	1.50				
	Manganese	.25/.40	O-1	Carbon	0.90	
	Silicon	.30/.50		Tungsten	.50	
	Chromium	11.50		Manganese	1.35	
	Molybdenum	1.00		Silicon	.35	
	Vanadium	.90		Chromium	.50	

through eighteen different steps in crafting a blade by the stock-removal method before he even gets to polishing or putting on a handle; and Bob Dozier does nine polishing operations just placing a finish on his blades, and even more during hand polishing.

Blade grind doesn't offer as many options as the other parts of a knife. There is a fair selection of grind available, but most cutlers do either a flat grind, resembling a V if you were to view a cross-section of the blade, or a hollow or semi-hollow grind, similar to a straight-edged razor. A number of so-called experts have voiced the view that a hollow grind has no place on a hunting knife because it weakens the blade. This is nonsense, for more hollow-ground blades are being offered by makers than any other style. Hollow grinding gives a special beauty to a knifeblade, and is used by most fine craftsmen; men like Loveless, Dowell, Hale, Horn and others grind exquisite hollow-ground blades and have never had one broken.

Regardless of the method utilized in crafting the blade, there are only two ways of fastening a handle to the completed blade, and that is with a full or narrow tang. Both enjoy equal popularity, with perhaps a slight edge going to the full tang at present. With this style of knife the tang generally follows the blade width and both sides of the steel are covered with scales or slabs of various materials. With the narrow tang, the tang is ground down and inserted into a handle that completely covers the tang. Proponents of the full tang feel it's stronger and presents the weight of the knife to the hand with a feeling of better control. Such a way of constructing a knife means all the mass of the handle is functional and contributes to the total strength. The narrow-tang knife, on the other hand, perhaps allows for a bit more room for the maker to exercise artistic design with curves and lines. While the full tang is undoubtedly stronger, a properly made narrow-tang knife can be more than sturdy enough. On the latter the tang is set into a hole in the base of the handle and held by pins, industrial epoxy and often a threaded butt cap or nut.

Argument arises over the weak point of the blade where it enters the handle and the tang is often at its narrowest. The reason for this disagreement is the sharp angle cuts made in the tang, or where a careless maker doesn't shape his cuts or even takes away too much steel. In fact, some narrow-tang knives are practically full-tang, so wide is the tang. Good craftsmen will not stint on materials or their ability, and Ted Dowell feels if the tang width is held to the maximum, as with the Morseth knife, for example, the narrow-tang knife is adequately strong.

With the exception of Loveless, most knifemakers offer both methods of finishing a knife. Certainly the exposed steel on a full-tang knife requires no more care than the blade, and properly sealed with epoxy and Micarta liners it won't rust. Some makers, including Loveless, brass-wrap the tang before adding slabs and final grinding. This is more for beauty than utility, but it does make a rustproof tang. I own and use both types and can report no difference in function or reliability. All are handsome, practical and functional. In fact, magnificent knives are crafted in both styles and the connoisseur should give himself the opportunity of owning one of each style and judge for himself.

Considering the weight of your knife you certainly don't want a great, hulking monster, and much will depend upon the type of handle material chosen and the thickness of steel stock used by the maker. Most knifesmiths select a bar ranging from $\frac{1}{8}$ to $\frac{1}{4}$ inches, depending on length of blade and intended use, to give the finished knife correct balance and permit efficient service. Basically there is no reason for a heavy knife, and most lightweight models serve splendidly. However, there are some men who prefer a brute of a knife, and if it feels comfortable and he knows how to use it, he should have a large knife.

What are the most important features of a good knife? John Nelson Cooper says, "The blade, no matter what its design, should have the ability to hold a good cutting edge. The next most important feature is balance—the knife should feel good in the hand of the user. Blade length is important also, but this is more dependent on each person's taste." Cooper is one of the elder statesmen of knifemaking and speaks from long years of experience.

I suggest you look around, decide exactly what you want in a knife and then order it. I bet you'll be amazed and slightly awed the first time you try your new knife, and that you'll agree that it was worth the wait, and the money, too.

chapter 3

what knife for you?

What's the best knife for you? That's like asking what wife is for you, or what shotgun or motor car. It all depends on your knowledge, experience and what you expect to get. But bear one thing in mind. There really is no such thing as an all-round knife, even though some utility blades come close. Any knife you choose must be a compromise of sorts, despite claims to the contrary and no one knife can do everything. Just as there is no all-purpose rifle or shotgun, though some calibers come close enough to suit most requirements, there is no all-purpose knife.

A knife is basically a working tool, despite the beauty of many specimens, and depending on the functions you wish it to perform, you may find it easy or hard to select the best style of knife or blade length for the job. Fortunately, the rules for selecting a knife are less complicated than picking a wife. And luckily a good knife may make a modest dent in your bankroll, but it won't bust you completely if you make an error of judgment. (In fact, many knife-makers will allow you a reasonable amount of time to fondle, caress and even use the goods before paying, which should satisfy the most demanding customer.)

Few men, experienced or not, ever agree on just what does constitute the best knife or blade style or length. For the question pops up, the best knife for what? Fishing is a prime example. Most fishermen prefer a fairly slim, flexible blade, but the fillet knife, while admirable for its intended use, is not much good for anything else. The man who shoots upland game is luckier. If he sticks with birds he won't need a knife longer than three or four inches,

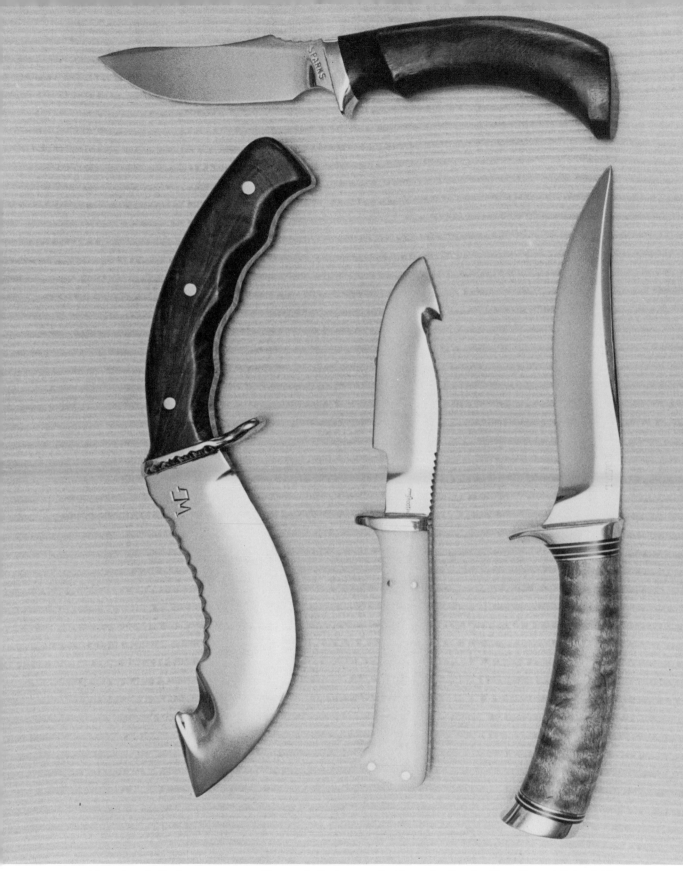

There is a knife for every taste. The top knife is a small skinner by Sparks. The others, left to right, are a large, wildly curved blade by Wayne Goddard with a gut-hook at the very tip; an ivory-handled knife by Lou Booth with gut-hook and an unusual finger cutout; and a general hunter with curly-maple handle by Dwight Towell.

and if he's good with a knife, he may use the same one on deer or larger game. Too often a man going out to buy a knife puts his money where his eye is, and ends up with a blade that gleams like a diamond in the showcase of the sporting goods store, but can't cut the mustard in the field.

Most sportsmen want a good, practical knife for field use. It should have a handle that's comfortable to hold and doesn't cramp the hand, and the blade should maintain its cutting edge.

Many different tasks are required of a knife. Simply gutting, skinning, quartering, boning and caping the average trophy would ideally require a half dozen different blade shapes. Obviously this is impractical, since no sportsman is expected to tote a cutlery department in his hip pocket. But you can't skin a mouse and a moose equally well with the same blade; you may try, but it can't be done efficiently.

If we were to analyze the thing a knife is most generally used for, skinning a deer for example, you'll appreciate the problems a knife designer sets for himself. The blade must be narrow enough to ream the anus, then have enough curve for skinning after you've opened the hide. The point must be sharp or tight enough to get under the belly skin without perforating the intestines. Each function would ideally require a different size and shape of blade. Yet the knifemaker has to come up with a design that will do everything at least pretty well.

Any knife you buy should be carefully selected for its intended use. Still, the variety of design, shape and blade length available is staggering to contemplate and confusing to behold. The problem is that everyone who picks up a knife and examines it for a few moments fancies himself a knife designer and knows instantly how it may be improved. But designing a knife isn't all that simple, and many of the weird and wonderful shapes you find among knives prove impractical in the field.

When Bo Randall introduced his famous Model No. 1 a few decades ago, this Bowie variation practically set the standards for knife design at the time. Now the style has changed and Loveless blades are setting the pace. Since Loveless is a fanatic on functional design, the emphasis has shifted: "If a knife is designed properly, you should end up with a knife you can use without thinking." Loveless is absolutely correct, since the effect of design, both blade and handle, on function can hardly be overstated. Still, different makers will always have differing ideas as to what is truly functional. Most new knifesmiths start off with fairly radical design ideas, but as they progress in their ability to craft a knife, they simmer down to those shapes that not only prove practical, but are generally accepted by their customers. Of course, knifemakers who are also hunters have the advantage of personal field experience.

The trend today, if it could be called that, is toward smaller, more functional knives. (Swinging a big blade from your hip may look rugged, but it marks you as a greenhorn.) Most knives, regardless of the maker, still come in a few basic styles: the drop-point popularized by Loveless; an upturned blade, usually for skinning if it has a generous curve; and the traditional straight blade. Of course, there will still be subtle variations in blade shape, reflecting the personality of the maker.

When it comes to the all-important decision of how long a blade you should

Small hunting knives. These are typical of the good general-purpose hunter with blades averaging 4 inches in length. From left to right: Frank Centofante knife with wood Micarta handle and full tang; John Owens stick-handle model with maple handle; Quinton "Red" Watson Sierra Hip Hugger with black Micarta grips; George Stone High Country model with Micarta handle; John Smith knife with Ivorite (an artificial ivory) handle; Morseth Ozark Hunter with leather grips and stag butt; Dwight Towell knife with wood Micarta handle; and Dan D drop-point hunter with ebony slabs.

buy, sportsmen may disagree, but most knifemakers feel their clients order a knife too long for their needs. Remember, a true hunting knife has one primary purpose—to cut meat. Ted Dowell refuses to list a blade longer than five inches on a knife to be used in the field, feeling that anything longer isn't a useful tool. (On special order Ted is delighted to craft a blade upwards of seven inches or more, but he regards them as space fillers to hang in your den.) Jimmy Lile reckons a man should get what he wants, but if he's asked, he is quick to state that four or five inches is sufficient for any North American big game.

Warren Page, shooting editor of *Field & Stream* magazine for twenty-five years and now president of the National Shooting Sports Foundation, is one of the most respected men in the outdoor field and his hunting experiences could add up to twenty lifetimes for most men. Page is also that rare sportsman who can skin and cape his own game. Asked his thoughts on what might be considered a general-purpose knife, or as close as one might come to such a blade, Page said, "I'd vote for a relatively light knife with a hollow-ground blade. It should be about four inches in length, and no more than four and a half inches at the absolute outside. I see no point in carrying a great machete to handle a job most penknives will do."

As his personal choice, Page now carries a lightweight model by Harvey Draper or a slightly heavier one by Clyde Fischer. Though the blades are four inches or less, they are quite capable of gutting an elk. "They will not quarter an elk," Page admits, "but when I'm after elk or any big game I carry a light folding saw or small hatchet in my saddlebag to do any rib cutting that may be necessary." Warren feels those hunters who burden themselves with ten inches of blade belong in the category of the man who carries a .375 Magnum against Alaskan brown bear and then straps on a .44 Magnum just in case. Some of Page's trophy-hunting friends lean toward carrying two knives, one of the general-purpose type and another specifically designed for skinning and caping.

In Page's experience not every guide has either the knowledge or skills to do a fine caping job, particularly with horned game and around the eyes and nostrils of heads, and any man who regards himself as a trophy hunter should have the ability to do the work himself and should carry the proper tools in his kit. The removal of a hide is no easy task, and the difference in ability means either a happy taxidermist or an enemy for life.

Page pointed out that those of us who've seen native skinners hack away at trophy game in Africa, with pangas sharpened on the nearest rock, may regard this emphasis on proper knives as rather ridiculous. "I admire their ability to do a remarkable job with primitive tools and not ruin the hide or trophy, but I feel they are still doing it the hard way," is how Page puts it.

Peter Wiley is a member of Camp Fire Club and a keen hunter. Wiley went to Zambia on safari last year and watched some skinners at work on a zebra he'd brought down for camp meat. Without a word he unsheathed his small Morseth knife and handed it to one of the natives. "The blade slipped through the hide like butter and the biggest grin I'd ever seen appeared on the face of the skinner."

Other makers are in general agreement. George Herron: "I think average blade length is a matter of personal opinion. I know some fellows who use a ten-inch knife. I can't, and feel four and a half inches is enough." Rod Chappel: "I like a small skinner, about three and a half inches long, so I can feel my way inside an animal. For all-round work? Five inches is enough." Ray Schmidt of Track Knives: "Four inches is a helluva lot of knife, but we'll make 'em any length the customer wants." John Smith: "The first knife I ever bought was an eight-inch skinner just like everyone else. When I began making knives, and learned about them, I found a four-inch blade is enough for any man."

There are exceptions, of course, and a couple that come to mind are Clyde Fischer's seven-inch Y.O. Special and Y.O. No. 1 models. These are specially designed knives for professional guides at the famed Y.O. Ranch at Mountain Home, Texas. Y.O. clients hunt trophy game, and these longer blades are favored for swiftly bleeding and field-dressing the animals. It is rarely, however, that an average hunter will require a blade of this size.

Bob Loveless, always generous in his admiration of good work, regards the Morseth Cascade skinner, designed by Harry's grandson Steve Morseth, as the most useful pure skinning design on the market today. Its blade is three and a half inches long. Another practical skinner is the Ozark Hunter; its blade is three and a quarter inches long, although it may be had on special order slightly longer.

When Harry Morseth passed on his grandson was making finer knives than

More general utility knives of various blade lengths. Left to right: Loveless drop-point with stag grips; Corbet Sigman knife with mother-of-pearl handle; L. B. Lienenmann knife with zebrawood handle; George Stone Diana model with stag slabs; Harvey Draper knife; and Bob Dozier new model with tapered tang and stag handle slabs.

the old man had dreamed of. Unfortunately he also tried to sell them for the same prices, and the result was financial disaster.

Andy Russell took over the firm in 1972 and kept a keen eye on design and eliminated some older models. While still retaining their distinctive three-piece stag handles and laminated-steel blades, Morseth Knives has added tapered tangs that allow more variety in design with flowing lines and brass-wrapped tangs—an extra goodie that makes many of these knives knockouts. Incidentally, Russell, at no small expense to himself, continued to honor all past orders for Morseth Knives to maintain the integrity of the company. Coming along late in 1973 will be an exclusive line crafted of three new steels to be known as Russell Super-Edge. All models will have integral hilts and will range in Rockwell hardness from 62 through 66.

For backpackers, George Stone has created an unusual blade called the High Country. It weighs in at an amazing four ounces, sans sheath, the result of removing material from the tang and guard area without loss of strength. The knife has a blade three and three-quarters inches long, and in combination with his Mini-Skinner and Trophy-Caper, it makes a compact trio of lightweight, easily carried knives. Another featherweight is Morseth's Ozark Hunter, with a backpacker's handle of wood Micarta, which also weighs under four ounces. Even Dan Dennehy has gone to shorter blades in his sportsman's line and admits to rethinking his entire approach to knives. A fine example is Dan's tiny Alpine hunter with a blade under four inches. It's a full-tang knife with slab sides of Philippine ironwood, and a man could be happy carrying this knife all day long.

In spite of the shrinking size of blades, there still exists a reasonable limit below which one should not go. I've seen a few very efficient blades no longer than two inches, but a knife is for cutting and you still need a certain amount of blade to cut with.

Lou Booth has perhaps come up with the ultimate in a pair of all-steel, self-handled blades. The longer, the utility knife blade, measures two and three-quarters inches and the rounded-belly model for skinning and caping measures two inches. Metal is removed from the handles for lightness, and each has thumb serrations atop the blade for a sure grip. These tiny blades can still do about any task you put them to.

Now that we've explored some of the different aspects of blade design, let's take a look at the other end of the knife. If the blade is the working end of a knife, the handle is the driving part, offering the knifemaker an even greater opportunity to display his talents as an artist. Many different materials can be used, singly or in combination, in making a knife's grip, hilt and pommel, and how these are put together will express both the taste of the maker and the discrimination of his client.

Caping knives are used by the experienced hunter for the intricate task of working about the eyes and nostrils of game and removing the cape. Left to right: Ted Dowell, Ralph Bone, Ron Lake, Lou Booth, Chubby Hueske.

These are small-bladed knives handy for birds, fish and small game, although in expert hands they are quite capable of skinning out deer. Left to right: Randall Model 8 Trout and Bird knife with stag handle; Lou Booth concept of the same style with unusual handle of crosscut zebrawood; Ron Lake bird knife with 3½-inch blade; Bob Loveless Lamb Utility, a recent try for a minimum working blade of 3¼ inches; and Jim Mustin bird knife with Osage-orange handle.

Probably the number one grip material on any maker's list is Micarta. A trademarked product of Westinghouse, Micarta is a phenolic resin compound that comes to the knifemaker in various textures and colors, including a handsome natural wood. The wood-base is probably the most attractive, but a slight edge for durability goes to the linen-base. The great advantage of Micarta is that it won't crack, shrink, warp, chip, burn or discolor. It's impervious to rain, humidity and dampness and practically indestructible. John Nelson Cooper, the noted Burbank knifemaker, feels so strongly about this material that he refuses to use any other for his sturdy knives.

Next to Micarta, the most popular grip material and the traditionalist's favorite is Indian sambar stag. This material combines strength and beauty, and the roughness of the horn gives a firm nonslip grip. Stag must be crafted with

Matched sets of blades, the lefthand pair by Track Knives and the other by Rod Chappel (Davis Custom Knives). Such sets should be able to undertake any task of skinning and caping trophy game.

Large hunters are popular with Western hunters and those who go after elk or moose. Left to right: Lou Booth knife with ivory Micarta handle; Ralph Bone knife with rosewood handle; Bernard Sparks knife with Indian stag grip; Don Zaccagnino Cougar custom with brass spacers and guard; and Weatherford Brothers Model #2 with stag handle and damascened blade, a Weatherford trademark.

a deft hand, since its natural density can easily lead to a handle that overpowers the blade in proportion or weight. Some craftsmen sand down the rough outer horn, removing all ridges until the stag presents the appearance of ivory.

For many years leather was the most commonly used material for knife handles, since scraps could be easily obtained from the nearest saddlemaker or shoe repairman. It is easily applied, shaped and machined. Problems arise with untreated leather, however, because it tends to absorb blood and body fluids from the animals and can take on an offensive odor. It can also dry out and shrink. These problems caused a gradual decline in the use of leather, and handles of this material almost passed from the scene until Harry Morseth developed a special process that eliminated rotting and shrinking while still providing an almost slip-free grip. Morseth Knives is one of the few makers that offers these specially treated handles, which Andy Russell, the new owner, will guarantee for the life of the owner. Many hunters still swear by leather-handled knives and say there is no better material in practice, particularly when you're working within the body cavity of an animal, because of the grip provided.

Rare woods, especially those from South America, Africa and Southeast Asia, have a beauty unequaled by any other material. The hardwoods—rosewood, cocobolo and lignum vitae—make unusual handles with their complicated patterns and delicate shades. The natural oils contained in these woods impart a sheen with long use and protect the wood from cracking. Walnut, teak, ebony, curly maple, vermilion, Australian brushbox and a host of others are also used for handles. (Unfortunately the ebonies, both Gaboon and Macassar, have a tendency to check or crack, and most makers prefer not to use them.)

Of course, there's nothing wrong with our native woods. Persimmon, cherry and oak make beautiful handles and are often used. Many knifemakers specialize in local woods of their area. Jim Mustin of Cajun Knives crafts unusual and striking handles from a wide selection of southern woods, ranging from honey locust to pecan, while Clyde Fischer is as famed for his handles of Texas mesquite as he is for fine blades. Fischer recently unearthed a treasure trove of oozuk, which is, believe it or not, a walrus' "family jewel." Oozuk is a hard, bonelike material that resembles aged ivory when brought to a high polish. It's unusually rare of course (walrus don't give it up willingly) and prices run high—about a hundred dollars on top of the charge for the knife. But if a collector prides himself on exotica (or erotica?) he wouldn't have to look further.

The principal really fancy materials for handles are ivory and buffalo horn, and though most makers offer them, they are quick to point out their vulnerability to checking and cracking. If you're insistent and willing to accept the risk, they'll use these materials, and they do indeed make handsome grips. However, of my four ivory-handled knives three have cracked. The fourth is still protected by daily doses of baby oil. On balance, I don't think they're worth the trouble.

The fanciest material of all is jade, the Indian potentate's choice in knife handles. Walter ("Blackie") Collins, for one, has used it (for the price of a small automobile). He's in no hurry to repeat the stunt because of the difficulty of cutting jade. Of course, if you produce enough green stuff of both kinds, you might persuade him to change his mind.

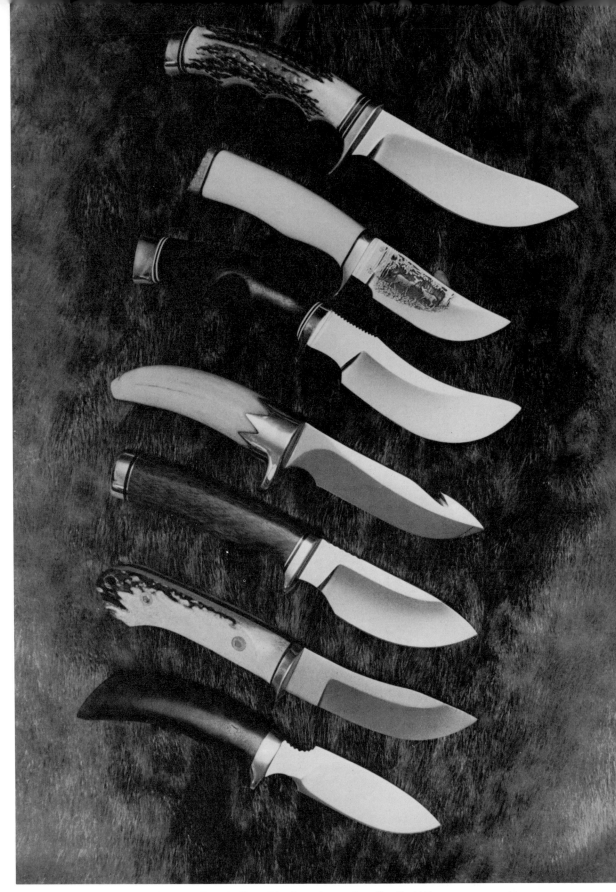

A range of skinners. Top to bottom: Dwight Towell knife with stag handle; Red Watson custom skinner with walrus-tusk grip and etched blade by Shaw-Leibowitz; Corbet Sigman skinner with rosewood handle; unique Jess Horn skinner with whaletooth handle; Ron Lake model with cocobolo handle; Frank Centofante full-tang model with stag handle; and George Herron's knife with Micarta grips.

More skinners. Top to bottom: Track Knives skinner with ivory Micarta handle; Rod Chappel skinner with wood Micarta grip; Lloyd Hale gut-hook skinner with handle of Dall sheephorn; Morseth skinner with cocobolo handle; John Smith Model 3, an excellent small-game knife, with stag grips; Bucker Gascon big-bladed skinner with Micarta handle; and Hibben model with stag handle.

Clyde Fischer knives. Left to right: Y.O. No. 1 with ivory handle and 7-inch blade; Rio Grande Skinner with stag handle; custom caper; and unusual small caper with oozuk handle.

The design aspect of the knife handle presents its own set of problems. Blackie Collins says that it's fairly simple to craft a beautiful knife, but that often it doesn't either feel right in your hand or work right. Collins has his own thoughts on handle design, and laughingly calls it the "Collins Edge Principle." What Collins tries to do is to visualize the edge of the blade and how it will be used. He then puts this edge in such relation to the hand that it will provide long use without becoming uncomfortable. Collins says, "Handle design should be thought of in terms of what an actual hand encloses in holding a knife. Envision, if you will, what the void is like when you clench your fist, and your ideas of handle design will change drastically." While the average knife handle might take up five cubic inches, the space inside your fist is nil.

Collins' best object lesson in handle design came about early in his career. An old lady in Louisiana wanted a knife for slicing vegetables, but her hands were badly crippled with arthritis. However, she knew exactly what the blade should be and insisted on designing the handle as well. Blackie began work, and every time he consulted his client she asked that more wood be shaved from the grip. More and more stock was removed until Collins feared he had ruined a fine piece of ebony. Surprisingly, however, as the handle became smaller it also became more practical and, Collins ruefully confesses, also grew in beauty. When the knife was completed they were both delighted and Collins says it gave him a never forgotten lesson in handle design: don't make them too big. More important, in Collins' view, he can't think of any situation where handle weight is of practical value on a knife designed for the field. Today the Collins Brothers (he works with brother Michael) are moving with the tide toward smaller knives.

Before beginning to craft a knife, many cutlers will ask for an outline drawing of your hand, as do certain pistol grip manufacturers, to ensure a proper grip. Don Zaccagnino offers small, medium and large handles. Rod Chappel requests your glove size and claims he's never missed yet. For your own guidance there are a couple of rules to follow. The handle should be long enough to cross your palm diagonally. If it does you'll find, when grasping the handle, there may be a spare half-inch or so protruding from the back of your fist. This is all to the good and will ensure a proper fit. Some makers prefer a slightly longer grip in the belief it allows the user more hand movement when working the blade. Some handles don't follow this rule at all since they are made to fit the palm of your hand. In this category fall certain boot knives and the small, skeletonized handles of certain specialized skinners or capers. There is, oddly enough, a difficult area of fit where a handle may be either too long or not long enough, or too short or not quite short enough. The best way, obviously, is to try to visit a knife show where you can handle the actual knives and select those that fit you best. For there is nothing worse than trying to do good work with a knife that doesn't fit. Flights of overworked imagination on the part of

A range of handles. From left to right: Sonneville hunter with ring guard; Clyde Fischer Osage-orange-handled Y.O. Hunter with finger grips; Jess Horn sub-hilt fighter; graceful Rod Chappel knife with choil; and Loveless knife with the Thomas Lamb improved handle.

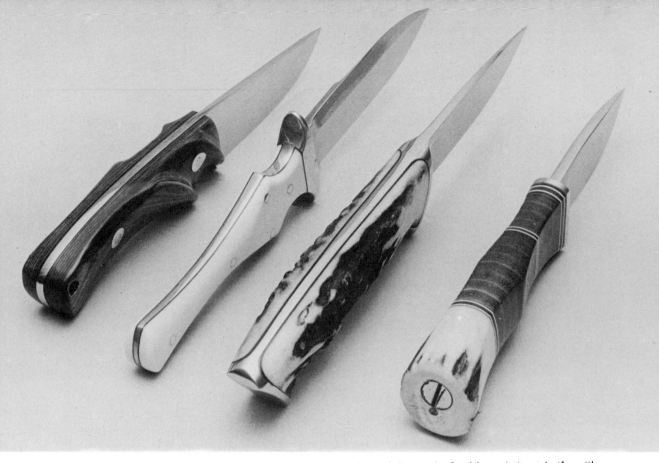

Various tang treatments. Left to right: Frank Centofante full-tang knife; Morseth boot knife with a brass-wrapped and tapered tang and ivory handle; Ted Dowell integral-hilt-and-butt model—blade, hilt and butt are machined from one piece of stock; and Morseth narrow-tang model with leather handle and stag butt.

Large and small, they all fill a demand for handmade knives. Top row, from left to right: Wayne Goddard with pistol grip handle; Bucker Gascon; Bernard Sparks; Lou Booth; Bob Dozier; and George Stone Magnum model. Bottom row: Frank Centofante Model 14; John Owens; Chubby Hueske Junior Texas with handle of pau ferro (a South American hardwood); and Don Zaccagnino skinner with stag handle.

Top to bottom: Don Zaccagnino large Cougar with lignum vitae handle, brass spacer and finger cutout on grip; Loveless small Dropped Hunter with 4-inch blade and stag slabs; and Rod Chappel Salmon River Utility-Hunter with cocobolo slabs.

Variations of blade shape and style. Top to bottom: Bob Dozier full-tang model with Osage-orange slabs; fine Ted Dowell knife with magnificent Eastern curly-maple handle; small Dan Dennehy knife with 3-inch blade and Philippine ironwood handle; handsome Lloyd Hale model with Dall sheephorn handle; and Morseth knife with purpleheart handle topped in typical fashion with an Indian stag butt.

a knifesmith may be handsome to view in a collection, but are nothing but trouble in the field.

Aside from fit, what else should you look for in a handle? How about all those finger grooves, choils, rings and subhilts? What you hang onto can become slippery and sweaty pretty fast, and you need a firm grip. In addition, you are constantly changing the position of your hand on the handle when skinning, and still require a solid grip for leverage. In my opinion the slab, full-tang handle is ideal. It offers the greatest resistance to movement within your hand and won't turn or twist. Andy Russell affirms that finger grooves are mostly for beauty. He says that if the knife is to be admired in a collection, then include the grooves, but if it's a "using" knife, avoid them. Andy went on, "If you must have something to adorn your grip one groove is better than four, but none is best of all."

Dan Dennehy is another craftsman who says, "I abhor finger grooves and consider them a gimmick without value. The instant your hand leaves the grooves the knife is uncomfortable." Don Zaccagnino splits the difference: "I don't like finger grooves all the way down the handle because you don't use a knife for pistol shooting." However, Zack provides one distinct groove for the index finger and slight shaping for placement of other fingers. Since Zack makes every effort to balance his knives on that finger the handle works out very well. I own a knife by Corbet Sigman with one groove or choil, find it comfortable in use, and can offer no objection. Again, that's one man's opinion.

Any handle should have fairly flat sides. If it's too round it tends to move in your hand and will soon tire you through your need to grip tighter as you work. If you still want something to ensure a more solid grip, particularly with a smooth material, either a gentle choil or the Loveless Improved handle is nearest to an ideal. The Loveless Improved handle was designed by Thomas Lamb, an industrial designer, some years ago as the perfect orthopedic grip to fit any hand. The slight choil effect, with gentle indents on both sides of the grip, provides comfortable placement for the forefinger and thumb and yet is not sharp enough to interfere with a constantly changing grip.

From blade and handles we move to workmanship. Some knifemakers may feel I overemphasize this point, but next to beauty and function, fine craftsmanship and finish are what knifemaking is all about for me. Most customers think they know what they like, but knowing what you like and what is good are two different things. A knife expert can pick up a knife, turn it over a few times and spot flaws in a flash. You may be surprised to learn he's quickly examined a dozen or more vital areas. You should learn to do the same; the ability to inspect a knife properly is essential to the knife buyer, for nothing else can protect you against shoddy work and a bad investment.

While it may appear we've been offering nothing but praise to the art of knifemaking, we must also report that some specimens are offered that might better be displayed in the trash bin.

Blackie Collins and Corbet Sigman are so protective of their customers that they have prepared a list of the key factors involved in judging a knife. It's an excellent check list, and on page 54 it is offered for your perusal with some personal additions.

A. Good and bad craftsmanship. The Ted Dowell knife shows an excellent fit of guard to blade. The fine silver solder is flawless, with no pinholes or rough edges. The other knife has too much silver solder and pinholes as well as poor polish.

B. The top knife, by Sigman, shows excellent polish and precise grind. The bottom knife, an effort of my own, is typical of the inexperienced maker, with uneven grind and poor finish.

C. Poor fit of guard to blade. Not only is there a lack of solder, but the guard is fastened at an angle rather than being straight across the center of the blade.

D. The knife handle on left is sloppy, with an excess of epoxy. On the right is a Loveless knife with well-fitted fiber liners and neat line of epoxy.

E. The false edge and bevel of top blade has an uneven grind and poor polish. Note how bevel lines do not meet. The bottom blade, by Corbet Sigman, has a fine bevel grind with exact meeting of both sides. This blade would truly reflect both sides if held in front of a mirror.

1. Does the blade have good lines, with sharp definition?

2. Are the bevels ground smoothly, without ripples or distortion?

3. Is epoxy or glue visible at the joints?

4. Is there excess solder where the guard is fitted, or pinholes indicating a poor solder job?

5. Is the blade functional and desirable?

6. Is the knife straight from end to end, and is the guard attached in the center of the blade when you hold it out and sight across it?

7. Is the blade straight, and the point in the center of the blade?

8. If the blade is mirror-finished, can you see coarse lines that weren't removed prior to mirror polishing? A true mirror finish won't show grinding lines and will reflect perfectly.

9. Is the entire knife cleanly finished, with no visible toolmarks?

10. Can you close your eyes and run a finger over the handle, spacers and butt and not tell where they meet?

11. Look carefully at one side of the blade, then the other. Do bevel lines terminate at the same point, or are they higher or lower on one side? One side of a properly made knife should be an exact mirror image of the other.

12. The most revealing way to inspect a knife is to look at it point first, that is, from the business end toward the butt. Flaws and poor quality will show up fast.

These may be demanding rules, but what we're discussing is the near-perfect standard most knifemakers set for themselves. Mind you, there will be minute flaws in any benchmade knife, since true perfection is impossible to attain, but most good cutlers strive for that pinnacle. Of course a knife could be deficient in every point listed and still serve its purpose, but if something is handmade it should not only look good but be flawless in execution. In my opinion workmanship will be the deciding factor for the greatest percentage

On the left is Ted Dowell's new Lightweight knife, basically a Model 10 in ⅛-inch thickness with fully tapered tang and ground with a thin and delicate cutting edge. Knife may be had with handle of either wood-base or linen-base Micarta. On the right is the improved handle of the new Morseth knife, available in exotic woods or Micarta.

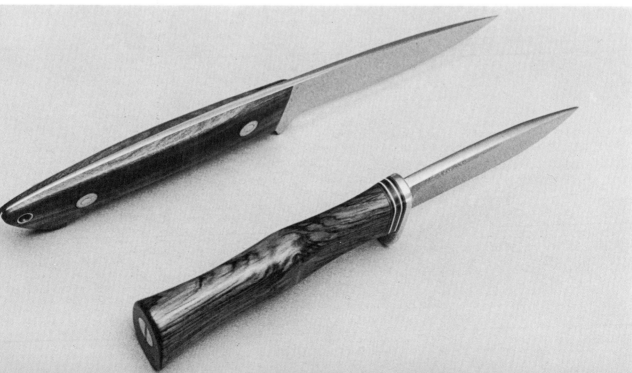

A fine selection of knives from various makers, all excellent all-purpose blades. Left to right: Loveless Straight Hunter with stag grip slabs; Wayne Goddard hunter with Osage-orange handle; Lloyd Hale model with Dall sheephorn handle; Merle Seguine model with handle of polished moose horn; John Smith's Model 7 with zebrawood handle and finger grooves; Sparks stag-handled knife; and Rod Chappel's Arctic Fox with cocobolo grip.

of future knife buyers. There was a time, a few short years ago, when any handmade knife would sell, but that's slowly changing as collectors and buyers become more expert and sophisticated in their tastes. Corbet Sigman once told me, "It's the last fifteen percent of the work that takes half the time. If you skimp on that final effort you'll never make an outstanding knife."

When it comes down the line to your final choice, knife buffs, hunters and just plain whittlers could argue until the coals of the campfire grow cold and never settle the question of the ideal knife. I'll put in my two cents and recommend that you buy the best knife you can afford, for a good blade is a lifetime investment. Properly tended, it may be handed down from father to son and give fine service for many generations. I own some forty knives and have used many in forays against grouse, trout and Arctic char—and even a mighty boar, brought down among the cork forests of Tunisia, that had the hide of a Sherman tank. So I feel I may speak with a modest air of authority. My personal preference is for a blade about four and a half inches in length with a slight drop point. I find this has sufficient cutting edge, cleans fish and birds well and is about the right length for camp chores or preparing meals.

I admit I'm no trophy hunter; I much prefer to sit in the shade of a tree, watching elephants pass in parade. Nonetheless, I've put in a fair number of years bashing about from the Amazon Basin through India, Malaya, Borneo and the highlands of New Guinea. In jungle areas I prefer a knife blade of 440-C since it stands up well in the humidity of the tropics. A small pocket stone keeps it sharp, and the short blade doesn't get in my way riding in Land Rovers, climbing into canoes or trying to adjust the myriad straps and buckles of airplanes or helicopters. I find this combination a practical knife for me. It does what I require, and that's all anyone can ask.

chapter 4

special-purpose knives

Special-purpose knives or knife variations can be called an exercise in imagination and design, a continuation of the knifemaker's constant search for a special blade or form that will handle a particular task a bit more efficiently than anything that has gone before.

Knives started out as fairly simple tools, but they're not ending up that way; specialization has been creeping in from all directions in the past few years. Some of Dan Dennehy's Eskimo-inspired Ooloo skinners are a perfect example. Derived from the circular or half-moon-shape tools used by the Eskimo to flesh hides from seals and walrus, these rather odd-looking blades actually do a splendid job; the results in use, at least in the hands of a professional, justify their curious appearance.

Blackie Collins, a highly regarded custom maker, keeps a constant flow of innovative ideas streaming from his Atlanta workshop. Just recently Collins created a trio of knives of quite revolutionary design which may be purchased separately or as a set. The knives are unusual in concept. Their skeletonized self-handles, orthopedically designed to fit the hand, are sculptured entirely of 440-C stainless steel which is vapor-honed (roughened) to prevent slippage. The knives are practically indestructible, and may be used for hours without fatigue. An advantage of the frame-type handle design is that the small weight-mass will quickly heat to hand temperature in cold weather. The three blade styles are calculated to provide scalpel-like efficiency and complete maneuverability even when the handles are wet.

The largest of the three, the Boat and Field model, was designed for all-

Top row, left to right: knives by Norman Dew; Lloyd Hale with whaletooth handle; Ralph Bone; and W. D. Randall, Jr.

Center row: George Stone Mini-Skinner and Trophy-Caper, plus a fillet knife; Cooper gut-hook skinner; Randall Survival knife with hollow handle; Chubby Hueske large knife; small Jim Mustin Micarta-handled skinner.

Bottom row: Bob Loveless Gentleman's Field Knife with ivory handle; George Herron small utility knife; Dan Dennehy Ooloo-type skinner; Hueske utility knife; Clyde Fischer Rio Grande skinner.

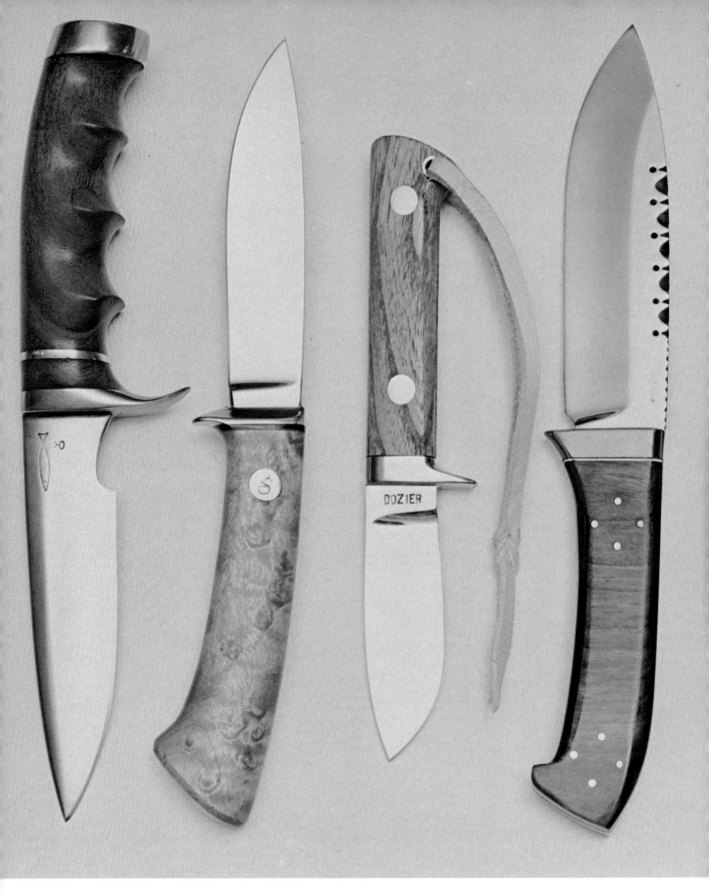

A colorful variety of handle materials is available to add distinction to your knife. Left to right: Clyde Fischer drop-point hunter with Texas mesquite handle; Ted Dowell model with bird's-eye maple; Bob Dozier small skinner with handle of Osage-orange; Lou Booth decorative blade with bubinga handle;

Bob Loveless knife with handle of Indian sambar stag; ornate Corbet Sigman knife with laminated handle of slabs of maple and cocobolo; Morseth knife with typical three-piece stag grips; Rod Chappel knife with beautifully grained cocobolo; and Lloyd Hale small Bowie with ivory slabs. All are handsome and the choice is yours—though Micarta is more durable than any of these materials.

From left to right: Arkansas toothpick with rosewood handle and Bowie with ivory grips by Lloyd Hale; modernistic Bowie by Rod Chappel with cocobolo handle and stainless-steel guard and butt cap.

The magnificent acid etching of Shaw-Leibowitz shown on three custom knives.

A selection of knives for around the water. At top is a Lloyd Hale custom fillet knife with rosewood slabs; below it a Ted Dowell all-steel (440-C) knife; on the right a George Herron Oyster Shucker; and at bottom a Randall Model 10 Salt Fisherman with nonslip grip and G. W. Stone Brook Trout Deluxe.

round utility use. Its blade is one inch wide and three and three-quarters inches in length. The wide, short blades of the two skinner models (both one and a half by two and a half inches) enable the user to control the point without having to move the hand or forefinger over the blade. However, should you prefer to work that way, the flat, wide spine allows the finger to ride well forward, ensuring absolute point control. The Trailing Point Skinner is for field-dressing large game and allows the hunter, working with the sharply pointed tip, some margin of error and a slower but surer access to the hide and cavity. This model might be recommended for the less experienced. The Leading Point Skinner can also be used for large game and caping, but should be regarded as the more professional of the two.

The knives come in an unusually flat sheath made from quality nine-ounce leather. The sheaths are unique in that they may be worn on narrow or wide belts or even tucked into a hip pocket. Each knife comes with a tough, braided-nylon lanyard that slips over the wrist when dressing game. This leaves the hands free, yet protects the knife from loss.

Of all the special knives the small, single-piece steel blade is regarded by many as the ultimate knife, a knife pared down to the absolute minimum without frills or fuss. Their sleek, efficient lines could put many of them in the running for design awards. The most popular slivers of steel are George Stone's miniature Trophy-Caper and Mini-Skinner. These blades may be purchased separately but are best bought as a kit since they complement each other so well. They are the exact opposite of Stone's regular knives, particularly his large Magnum Hunter, and are solely for skinning and caping game. The knives don't

57

have true handles as such, rather finger grips along the blade extension. They let you work with the precise and delicate control of a surgeon. A couple of inches of steel, honed to a scalpel-like sharpness and tucked into a sheath the size of the average key case, will do any skinning job you set them to.

Bob Dozier usually prefers doing custom work, but he, too, has tried his hand at the small, self-handled specialized skinner. Like most knives of this genre, "it may be hell for looks, but it's also hell for good," as a fellow once said. A slim knife with a three-inch blade, vapor-honed its entire length, it could probably remove your appendix if you didn't want to use it for fish or game. Another variation is the Weatherford Brothers' small, two-inch blade with tiny gut-hook. The handle curves around your two forefingers while your thumb presses against the quarter-inch back. The whole thing makes one of the neatest fish knives I've ever seen, and it could certainly also be used on birds and small game. In the Weatherford tradition, the entire knife is damascened, giving it a striking appearance.

The purist fisherman who hasn't the least interest in stalking anything except his finned friends hasn't been neglected by the fancy knife crowd. Chappel, Dozier, Dowell, George Stone and others offer the aficionados of the fly some excellent knives for their sport. Rod Chappel designed a beautifully made, slim-bladed knife with magnificent handles of stag or cocobolo. It's called the Coeur d'Alene and its lines are as graceful as a trout coursing slowly upstream. Bill Sonneville has a model named the Bonita that comes with either a six-inch or seven-inch blade with a scaler on back. Crafted of 440-C, it's an excellent knife for the saltwater fisherman. Another is his Barracuda, a larger version that's ideal for deep-water work and sturdy enough (if you want to jump overboard) for a hand-to-hand battle with a marlin or tarpon. This model is long and heavy enough to fillet large fish and could certainly sever the spine of the biggest monster of the sea. George Stone delivers three knives for the angler, ranging from the nine-and-a-half-inch narrow-bladed Marlin to the smaller and trimmer blade called the Brook Trout. I'll let you guess what they're suited for.

Ted Dowell has also come up with a slick marine knife designed for use around salt water while retaining his familiar blade shape. He, too, chooses 440-C and follows the trend with a self-handle and vapor-honing over the grip in this sleek addition to his stable of knives. The trimmest angler's knife is probably Randall's Model 10, the Salt Fisherman. The blade is not forged, as are most of Randall's knives, but hand-ground from high-carbon stainless with a handle of Duralumin or Micarta. The knife has deeply cut thumb serrations where blade and handle join and is crafted from eighth-inch stock, ground down to a slim and usable knife.

Bob Dozier, too, can provide you with a knife designed for salt water use. For the prosaic task of cleaning fish, it's probably as elegant a blade as a fisherman could choose to carry. Bob hollow-grinds the blade and uses green Micarta for the handle. John Smith is another who offers an exquisite fillet knife.

Overleaf: All-metal knives. Left to right: Bob Dozier small utility model; Hibben ring knife; three models of skeletonized-handle knives by Blackie Collins; another variation by Rod Chappel; Blackie Collins underwater model; Bob Dozier underwater model; and Weatherford Brothers tiny finger-grip gut-hook skinner.

It has the usual slim blade but is topped off with crown staghorn for the handle and is fine enough to place in a collection.

Now let's make a quick dive and take a look *under* the water. Blackie Collins and Dozier have both come up with similar radical diver's knives. (Although working hundreds of miles apart, two men can come up with the same idea at practically the same time.) Both are made of one piece of stainless steel, vapor-honed to cut down reflection and give a positive grip underwater. Collins' blade is seven inches long, Dozier's five inches long. Both have a row of sawteeth atop the spine of the blade for cutting rope and performing other difficult tasks underwater, and there are large circular flow vents in the handle to eliminate planing and permit rapid movement through water without unnecessary deflection or drag. Collins adds a pry claw at the end of his handle that could be handy for collecting abalone or coral or even extricating yourself from a tough spot while exploring old wrecks or treasure hunting. Sheaths of polyurethane are designed to be worn at the waist or on the leg. The material will not stretch or puncture with normal use.

These sensible and well-conceived knives could be an asset to any skindiver or underwater explorer who has had to struggle with the clumsy commercial products of the past. In fact, these sturdy knives would even come in handy as survival knives, and either would be excellent to place in an emergency kit or camping outfit. The Collins knife is named the Chael III, and Dozier calls

More fish knives. Top to bottom: Bill Sonneville Bonita fishing knife of stainless steel; John Smith fillet knife with crown stag handle; Bob Dozier model with green Micarta slabs; and Rod Chappel Coeur d'Alene fish knife with Indian sambar stag grip.

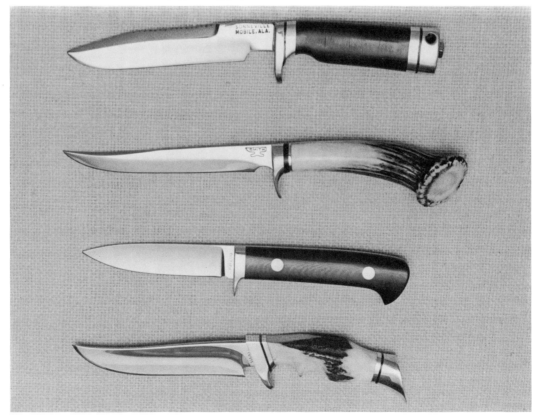

his the Underwater Knife. Both are special order items which may be modified on request.

For many knife buffs, the throwing knife has a special fascination, and few kids are able to resist the urge to hurl a knife—any knife—at some target and watch the blade clunk into the wood. Naturally this is the worst treatment you can give a knife unless it has been specially balanced and crafted for the sport. Fortunately, a great many knifesmiths craft special throwing knives, including Andy Russell, Blackie Collins and John Cooper.

In Collins' shop throwing blades have always been big items, and Collins has often tried to figure out why. Perhaps throwing a knife seems an especially manly thing to do, a sort of carryover from our pioneer heritage. Collins once mused, "If I had the guts to set up a target at a knife show and throw knives I'd probably sell more throwing knives than I could make in a year. But though it's nice to hear that resounding thump when a knife sticks in, it would be awful to have spectators watch your knife whack the target sideways, or miss it altogether." Collins told me that nobody has ever entered his shop who didn't want to play with his regular throwing knives. Young or old, male or female, the reaction is the same.

All makers who sell throwing knives emphasize the sport or hobby aspect and advise against ever tossing a knife in combat. (Never throw away your only weapon!) Throwing knives must be perfectly balanced, and if you want to hit something, you must know the target distance as well as how many rotations your knife will make before striking the target. And of course you *must* have a safe practice area.

There are many techniques in knife throwing, but this isn't the place to try to describe them all. As a fellow who has trouble balancing a checkbook, I stick with the trial-and-error method of most knife throwers, which means shuffling your feet back and forth a couple of inches after each throw until the knife sticks in. Those specially interested in throwing should write Harry K. McEvoy, whose address is in the appendix. McEvoy has been making throwing knives for over twenty years, has written a fine book on the subject and is the acknowledged expert in the field.

As the illustrations show, most throwers don't have guards. Guards are desirable in many knives but a thrower wants nothing to break the knife's symmetry of line or interfere with its flight through the air. Good throwing knives are relatively inexpensive compared to other handmade knives, usually costing $25 or less, and they are a worthwhile investment if you can't overcome the temptation to toss a blade. Should you decide to get a throwing knife, let me offer a word of advice: stay away from the cheap imports. Most of them are too light for serious use and are known as "floaters" by the experts. Like most other handmade items in the knife field the best would be cheap at double the price.

Perhaps the most innovative recent idea in knife design is the gut-hook, attributed to Merle Seguine of Juneau, Alaska, and his friend Sid Bell. Bell, now famed for his splendid sports jewelry, was once a geologist with the Bureau of Mines in Alaska and would sit about Seguine's shop talking knives and hunting. One evening, as Bell tells it, they were discussing the difficulty of skinning game and thought how great it might be if animals had zippers

Harry McEvoy's Tru-Balance throwers. These are hand-crafted of specially tempered spring steel. The center model is a true professional throwing model.

More throwers. From top to bottom these are by Randall, Dan Dennehy, Hibben, Cooper and Russell.

on their stomachs. Seguine segued right from this to the concept of the gut-hook. Since then his original concept has been copied by many knifemakers and adapted for everything from small blades to parachute jumpers' models for slicing shroud lines. Although some men swear by them, the gut-hook isn't a knife I favor. My main objection is the fact that it is a fairly dangerous knife with that nasty razor hook on the backside, and more than normal caution must be exercised in use. In addition, the hook is a fair devil to sharpen. Most men I've talked to delight in using the hook, but despair in sharpening it. However, I don't mean to downgrade Seguine's contribution to special-purpose blades.

There aren't many specialities that have been ignored by custom cutlers. The prize for the most unusual piece of special-purpose cutlery has to go to George Herron, who has concocted a knife for shucking oysters. If you want one just order his Model 10. Although crafted for a fairly mundane task, the knife is built with all the care and precision of Herron's regular knives. A unique triple-sided brass guard protects the hands against the sharpest shells, a Micarta handle with finger grooves gives firm support (this is one place the grooves work well) and the sturdy four-inch blade has got to be one of the strongest in the business—for the work at hand it better be.

Unless you're a muzzleloading enthusiast, you may well wonder what the hell a patch knife is used for. No, it's not for cutting patches when your wife sews up a worn pair of hunting trousers. Before the rifle ball is rammed home in a muzzleloading arm, it is wrapped with a small piece of cloth or patch and the excess is cut off at the muzzle for a smooth fit. The patch knife is short-bladed, usually around three and a half inches in length, and ground flat on one side in order to cut smoothly across the muzzle of the gun. Among the knifemakers who specialize in this unusual blade for the black-powder buffs are Ralph Bone, Wayne Goddard, H. G. Bourne of Wheeler-Holmes and Bill

The ultimate in small capers and skinners. At top, Wayne Goddard small skinner and Lou Booth model with tiny gut-hook; at bottom, George Stone Mini-Skinner and Trophy-Caper.

A fine pride of knives from H. G. Bourne. From left to right: Bowie made in the classic style with hammer marks still showing on the blade; fighting knife with Micarta handle; fighting-survival blade with hollow handle and O-ring, stiletto with hollow handle; a muzzleloader's patch knife; and push dagger.

Moran. They all do fine work on a knife that simplifies a difficult job. Walter Kneubuhler also makes a handsome model, in the traditional manner of the Old West, but it's sold only as a complete set along with his authentic hunting bags that include flint strikers, chargers and touch-hole pick. For muzzleloading fans, Walter's accessories lend a touch of realism.

Kneubuhler, a flintlock enthusiast himself, has long been fascinated by the era of the early west of the mountain men, and works exclusively in this romantic period of history. Although crafting a fine series of knives that can be used for many hunting purposes, Walter prefers to identify with the frontiersmen while advertising himself as "Walter Kneubuhler's Mountain Man Supplies, Fine Hand-Made Knives and Other Possibles" (those "other possibles" including tomahawks, for example). Walt's intimate knowledge of those early days, resulting from a formidable amount of research, has enabled him to craft superb reproductions. In fact, I doubt that any man of the fur trade ever carried knives as fine as Kneubuhler's. His most famous knife, the Mountain Man, was named to honor those rugged individuals who roamed the high country seeking their fortune in beaver plews (as the pelts were called in those days) and had a close association with Indians of the plains.

Walter was probably born a century and a half too late in time and projects the outward appearance of his predecessors. Gruff and hardy, he affects fringed jackets and a salty-looking western hat with an eagle feather stuck in the band. Under this impressive facade you find a kindly, gentle man, willing to share his tremendous range of knowledge with all comers. All of his products are designated by names made famous by the French voyageurs, explorers and trappers and conjure up visions of shining mountains and passes where the winds howl and snow drifts down through thick pine boughs: Wind River, South Pass, Grand Teton and Bayou Salade were all famous hunting grounds and gathering places of the mountain men.

Of all Kneubuhler's knives perhaps the most picturesque is the Blackfoot Dag of the high plains. This is a copy of the blade supplied the Hudson's Bay Company by the English firms of Sorby & Company and Jukes Coulson & Company of Sheffield. The shape of the blade obviously enjoyed great favor with the tribes of the Northern Plains near the Rocky Mountains, and the Blackfeet, Piegans, Bloods and Assiniboins used it with great fervor. Of all the handle materials used by modern knifesmiths Kneubuhler, in his Blackfoot Dag, has the most unusual—the six-inch blade is topped with a real bear or wolf jaw handle with the rows of teeth left on for a solid grip.

The sheath of this unusual knife is soft, smoke-tanned moose or elk skin, tanned in the traditional manner and decorated with beadwork and long fringe. The only concession to modern practicality is a fiber insert, like Morseth's, to keep the blade from punching through the leather. Walter doesn't stint on materials, using hand-forged blades of high-carbon steel with German-silver guards. A collector who doesn't have a Kneubuhler knife is missing an opportunity to own an authentic and colorful piece of Americana.

Bill Moran of Frederick, Maryland, may be the greatest traditionalist of all, since he sometimes crafts his knives in the style of the ancient armorers with hammer and forge and has explored the secrets of the olden Damascus blades. Moran considers that the last fine Damascus blades were made by Paul

Left to right: Morseth Pilot-Parachutist-Survival knife with purpleheart handle and stag butt; Randall Model 17, the famed Astro knife designed by Major Gordon Cooper; Randall Model 16 Diver's knife; John N. Cooper Barracuda underwater knife; Loveless parachute knife made as an emergency jumper's knife and survival tool; Cooper Shawnee model, a skydiver's and yachtsman's knife.

Mueller, a German who produced presentation daggers for high-ranking Nazi officials. The Nazi party set up a school in the city of Dachau with Mueller and seven pupils. The blades were forged exactly as the originals and Mueller's work was outstanding, although little known today.

Moran uses the same methods, beginning with a steel and iron weld, heating, folding and then drawing the bar out a bit. Then it's heated and folded again and again until there are more than a thousand layers of steel. Moran's reproductions of daggers and poignards of the Renaissance period are his most unusual work, taking hundreds of hours to craft. His greatest fame lies in his classical blades, and he's the only maker who crafts them in their original combat quality. In addition to his stilettos and poignards of steel, he also makes the great *cinquedea,* a replica of the knife carried by Cesare Borgia and other nobility of the Italian Renaissance.

Bill has devoted a lifetime to research on the subject of early iron and steel work, and frequently lectures on the ancient methods of blacksmithing. He tempers his own blades, using the same techniques as the bladesmiths of the seventeenth century. Since these methods are so little known today, a brief description might be in order for those interested in the subject. The bar of steel is first heated in a fieldstone forge, then slowly hammered into shape. Each blade is heated and hammered and reheated and reforged dozens of

The picturesque regalia of Walter Kneubuhler. From left to right: hunting bag with patch knife, horn, flints and striker; the Bayou Salade, a skinner named after a great gathering place for buffalo; the Mountain Man, etched by Shaw-Leibowitz with sheath fashioned in the old style and designed to be

worn over the outer garment; and the famed Blackfoot Dag, a double-edged blade of the type traded by Hudson's Bay Company to High Plains Indians, with an unusual handle made from a black bear jaw with teeth intact and a sheath of smoke-tanned moose or elk, richly decorated.

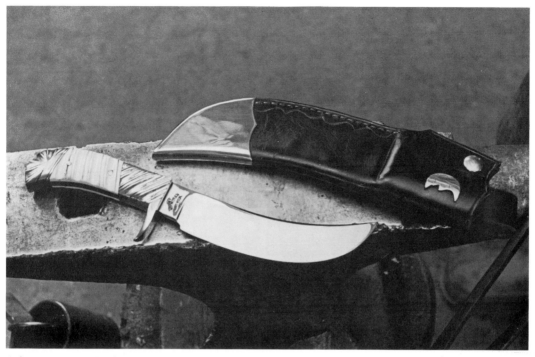

A fine skinner with silver-and-ivory handle by Bill Moran.

times before this part of the operation is complete. The blade is then ground by hand to near final shape and painstakingly hand-tempered by eye and hand in the forge. This tempering gives the steel special qualities which, Bill claims, no other modern hand-forged steel possesses. Moran's blades are very hard from the center to the edge. The back of the blade is tempered to about the consistency of a spring. The point is slightly less hard than the edge, while the tang is annealed for maximum tensile strength. Such unique tempering results in a blade that combines strength and edge-holding ability to a degree unattainable by any production-line method. Moran's blades have to be tempered by hand; they cannot be tempered in a furnace because each part of the blade requires a different degree of heat.

Following tempering, the blade is ground to a mirror finish; you really see your face in a new Moran blade. The handle and mountings are also made by hand, then fitted, shaped and sanded. Every technique is used that will make the finished unit as solid as possible. When the knife is completed the blade is hand-honed and stropped.

Moran's *cinquedea* is the most complex form of dagger. The handle alone contains twenty-six pieces. The edges of the tang are bound in brass, and the guard and pommel and all mountings are hand-cut from solid brass bar-stock. The sheath itself is nearly as complex, and complements the unusual blade with a brass tip, throat and belt stud. With his latest interest in recreating the Damascus blades, Moran's research may take him into many new areas. Fortunately he is a peaceful man, and has decided against the legendary method of tempering Damascus blades: running them through human bodies.

Opposite: Bill Moran at his forge hammering a hot blade into shape.

71

Of his regular knives Moran offers Bowies, combat knives and general hunting blades. Most of his regular knives are made of quarter-inch stock; in his opinion, three-eighths-inch stock is too thick and wedge-shaped for ordinary use and doesn't cut or slice well. (I can hear the screams from the competition, but as I've said all along, every man is entitled to his opinion.) Moran must be doing something right, since he's backed up *four years* on delivery.

One of the outstanding men in knifemaking, John Nelson Cooper, crafted his first knife when he was nine years old. (It took him something like thirty days.) As he grew older Cooper continued to make knives, although he became a welder by trade, and even in the Air Force, serving in the Panama Canal Zone, he still made knives for friends in off-hours. After discharge Cooper set up shop in Virginia Beach and seriously began to design knives for different uses. His first semi-professional effort, for a Korea-bound G.I., led to a wide selection of fighting knives.

Some twelve years ago Cooper retired from welding and moved to California, where he joined forces with nephew George Cooper and Don Nagel, both actors, to form Cooper Knives. The group now offers more than forty different models covering almost every conceivable requirement of the knife user. His special-purpose blades run the gamut: throwing knives, a gut-hook parachutist model, even an exact reproduction of the kukri, the famed fighting knife of the Gurkhas of Nepal. Situated in the heart of movieland in "beautiful downtown Burbank," as John likes to boast, he naturally undertakes many special projects for the movie and television industries. His knives have probably slit the throats of more enemy soldiers (before the cameras, that is) than all other makes combined. Among the sportsmen actors who boast Cooper hunting knives are Bob Stack, Clint Eastwood and Lee Marvin.

An unusual feature of Cooper's knives is that their joints are all bonded together, so that they become virtually one piece. Cooper holds a number of U.S. patents on this process, which eliminates all spaces or recesses in which blood or other fluids might build up and cause oxidation.

If you require a particular blade no craftsman has yet conceived, most cutlers are happy to listen to your ideas and quote prices on your sketch. I know one man, a police officer, who keeps a small gut-hook accessible in his car to slice the seat harness if he should crash or roll over in a high-speed pursuit. He remembers with horror the charred body of one accident victim who could have escaped if a knife had been handy.

Not really a special-purpose knife but certainly in the family is the small hand axe many hunters carry, and a number of excellent knifemakers have begun to turn out small custom axes to carry in a pack or saddle bag. Ted Dowell has made axes for many years and shows them in his catalog. They are made with the same care as his knives. They are crafted from a single piece of Staminal steel with a maximum head thickness of three-eighths of an inch and handles ground from one-quarter inch and tapering down to one-sixteenth at the butt. Ted's steel is about 30 percent tougher than standard S-5 (shock-resistant steel used for making pneumatic chisels and other large blades) and is hardened to about Rockwell 57-58. One of the unusual inconsistencies Dowell has found in steels is that over the years he's made axes from half a dozen different steels—5160, O-1, A-2, S-5 and others—and while these

Three of Moran's classical knives. On the left is a stiletto in the style of the 17th century. It is forged of three pieces of steel—handle, guard and blade. The blade is about 7 inches long. In the center is another classic dagger, of a type used in the 16th century. It is also forged of steel, and the blade is about 10 inches long. The knife on the right is a variation of the stiletto; the blade is roughly 9 inches long. Although Bill Moran has been crafting blades in Frederick, Md., for a number of years he still retains his old trademark of Lime Kiln, Md.

A wide range of Moran knives in front of the forge: two skinners, an Arkansas toothpick, a Bowie, and a patch knife with crown stag handle.

74

Matched knives and small trail axes. The pair at the top is by Ted Dowell, the other by Lou Booth.

A selection of small axes. The top axe is the Ridge Runner by Morseth. The others, left to right, are by Rod Chappel, Wayne Goddard, Ted Dowell, Don Zaccagnino, Jimmy Lile and Gil Hibben.

A variety of shapes and sizes from a single maker, Jimmy Lile. Top to bottom: a general-purpose blade with rosewood handle; Model 8, a small skinner; Model 9, known as the Elk; and a small drop-point hunter with walnut handle.

all will make excellent light axes, none will make what he considers a fine knife.

Jimmy Lile makes the usual type of small axe, and it's a real beauty, but more unusual is his cutting tool axe that resembles a small cleaver with gut-hook. Lile hasn't given it a name yet, but I'm certain if you ask for his cleaver-axe he'll know what you mean.

Rod Chappel and Lou Booth also make fine, lightweight axes. Booth crafts the most unusual shape of all. A curved blade with a hook on top and the sharpened edge running around to the front has to make this an all-inclusive axe. It will chop, rip, cut and slice, and while it may require more than normal care in handling it does make a proficient instrument. Booth, like Dowell, pairs it with a matching knife, and axe and knife together should handle any game on the North American continent. For hunting or survival these small custom camp axes take up little space in a pack, and while they are luxury items at their prices, they can make your job easier in the woods. Other makers who offer small axes include Morseth, Zaccagnino and Wayne Goddard.

The justification for any cutting instrument is that it work well when needed. If some of these special-purpose blades seem a bit farfetched, remember that we all don't have the same hobbies or interests. The hunter's use for his knife doesn't concern an explorer struggling to cut a rope in gale-force winds atop some Himalayan peak. Nor does the man who can spend five minutes to load and prime his powder burner care about some skindiver entangled in a kelp bed off the California coast. Special-purpose knives are primarily accessories for fun and pleasure, but some can be lifesaving tools in emergency situations. It might be worth a few moments of your time to ponder whether or not you have use for some special-purpose knife.

chapter 5

fighting knives

Fighting knives are among the most highly developed blades of all, and thus perhaps they should be classified with the other special-purpose knives. However, they have so many variations in form, along with their cousins, survival and boot knives, that they rate a section of their own.

If you're protesting that any old knife can be used for killing you'd be right; probably more kitchen knives have been used for mayhem than any other. However, when we talk about a true killing knife, a blade designed for that one specific purpose, we're dealing with a different matter entirely.

Fighting knives seem to have a very special look about them. Where other blades, particularly hunting or fishing knives, don't look particularly sinister, an efficiently designed fighting blade somehow appears to be waiting for something to happen, like a coiled rattlesnake. People who have been around knives most of their lives all change their expressions when you hand them a fighter or a nasty-looking boot knife. Perhaps when we handle a knife specifically made for killing another human being, atavistic thoughts pass through our minds, while other knives (hunting knives, for example) seem more friendly, reminding us of camping trips and successful hunts. To most Americans killing with a knife is repugnant, even though our early history ran red with the blood drawn by edged weaponry. Still, we find the knives themselves fascinating.

Even those who have occasion to put fighting knives to use may respond to them emotionally. I knew a two-man C.I.A. team operating in Southeast Asia. One agent was a knife buff who truly loved the blades. He carried enough knives about his person to stock a small shop, and had used most of them,

too. His partner hated knives and refused to carry one; he said if he couldn't get out of a scrape without using a knife, the hell with it!

Most killing knives originated in agriculturally based societies. The long, slim bolo of the Philippines came from the cane fields yet became a favorite weapon of Moro pirates and every fanatical Moslem who hoped to attain paradise by running amok and slicing his nearest neighbor.

Farmers in Latin America use a machete for every imaginable purpose. From my own experiences in the jungle I can say without reservation there isn't a tool like it anywhere. You hang it on your belt in the morning and it stays there until the day's work is finished. It's used for everything from pushing palm fronds aside as you walk through the jungle to giving a sharp rap to a log before stepping over it, chasing any lurking bushmaster or fer-de-lance. On one occasion, when an aggressive anaconda tried to slither into a stalled outboard motor boat, my companion and I hacked away with our machetes until the reptile gave up the fight. (I doubt if we killed him since it was like cutting a steel cable.) In any case, any junglewise expert would sooner go barefoot, and would be safer, than go without his machete. It's an all-purpose working and survival tool.

Probably the most renowned fighting knife in the world is the kukri, the wickedly curved knife of the Gurkhas of Nepal. Wherever these British-trained mountain men have gone into battle, their kukris have carved a wide swath among the enemy. Some years ago, when I worked in Malaysia, I went on an occasional patrol with the famed British Tracker-Killer Teams in Malaya and the Borneo States. The mission of these skilled jungle experts was to move into the jungle and keep pressure on enemy guerrillas, eventually tracking them to their hideouts and destroying them. The small, mobile groups, usually no more than a dozen men, were composed of Gurkhas with their tracker and killer dogs, British NCOs and Iban headhunters from Borneo. The Ibans and Gurkhas had much in common. They loved knives. During rest periods in the jungle they would unsheathe their blades and gently test the edge with their thumb, knowing all the time, of course, just how sharp they were. Whenever action seemed imminent, even though they were armed with the small Sterling gun, they would draw their kukris.

A perfect example of this reliance on knives was demonstrated one morning. Nearing a small native village that reportedly harbored guerrillas, two Gurkhas—a scout and his safety man—moved with the grace and elegance of ballet dancers from bush to tree, ever nearer to a lone hut in the clearing. Placing his gun on the ground, one soldier took two concussion grenades from his belt and hung them from his teeth. Then, drawing his kukri, he ran like a flash and vaulted through an open window, jumped out the far side and tumbled into the jungle, leaving the grenades inside. The roof seemed to lift off a few feet and drop down again. Two very frightened Indonesians ran out to face a yelling horde of snarling dogs, soldiers and wildly painted headhunters. There was no question of a fight, since orders were to take the enemy alive, and everybody was reasonably happy (except the Ibans, who wanted heads).

Often the mere sight of an unsheathed kukri is enough to discourage any further action by causing a cold, cramped feeling in the nether regions of the stomach. In fact some years ago a show of kukris aborted a revolt before it turned into a full-fledged revolution. We must go back some years to when the Federation of Malaysia was being formed after the Second World War. At that time the Sultanate of Brunei decided to remain under British protection, even though independent. (After all, they had all the oil.) A small enclave, Brunei sits comfortably along the lush jungle coast of Borneo (now Sabah) between Sarawak to the south and what was formerly Jesselton in British North Borneo.

Once while His Highness was on annual holiday in England, far removed from political intrigues and palace coups, an uprising was attempted. British military headquarters, then stationed in Kuching, the capital of Sarawak, was alerted and quickly flew a company of Gurkhas the short distance up the coast. Landing at Brunei airport, the little brown men double-timed into Bruneitown and soon came in view of the rioters.

Forming a thin khaki line across the lone main street, they unsheathed their kukris and stood facing the howling mob. Looking at that silent row of men, their knives sparkling in the sun, the insurgents had some fast second thoughts and slowly began to disband. The troops smartly about-faced, trotted back to the airfield and flew home to Kuching. Elapsed time to crush a rebellion—under two hours.

Anyone who has spent time in Southeast Asia soon comes to know the kris with its characteristic wavy blade. The national weapon of the Malaysian and Indonesian people, its history is probably the bloodiest of all fighting knives. The kris varies considerably in length, from the swordlike Kris Sudang of Borneo to the smaller variety, six to nine inches long. It's not easy to identify the origin of any kris; the blade could come from the small village of Khota Baru in up-country Malaysia, the handle from Sumatra and the sheath from any one of a dozen different islands. Basically the kris is a double-edged dagger or rapier, designed primarily for thrusting. The more waves in a blade (always an odd number) the greater its power in battle. No native weapon is more involved in superstition than the kris. Some believe you can kill a man just by pointing a certain magical kris at him, and the Malay greatly fears this power. It is also said that certain very powerful blades have the ability to jump out of their scabbards under their own power and fight in defense of their owner. This is not surprising, considering that most legendary krises were created by great craftsmen, forging the red-hot metal by finger pressure alone.

During the First World War the "trench knife," with its triangular blade and "knuckle-duster" guard, became the first modern knife especially designed for close combat in trench warfare. The Second World War and the Korean conflict saw military fighting knives come into their own, and Vietnam witnessed a wholesale introduction of handmade fighting knives.

When the British first introduced the Sykes-Fairbairn, a knife designed by E. A. Sykes and W. E. Fairbairn of Shanghai Police and British Commando fame, it was considered the ultimate killing knife. The original Sykes-Fairbairn was a slim, delicate, double-edged blade, one inch wide and a hair under seven inches in length. Its handle was serrated for a firm grip, and the blade was blued to cut reflections at night. For its purpose it had everything it needed and no faults, or so it seemed. Yet, in spite of its deadly appearance, it proved

too slim and fragile in use; if you were foolhardy enough to attempt anything more strenuous than slashing a throat or stabbing a kidney, the blade tended to snap off at the guard. It was a knife for stealth rather than combat, and most were relegated to the status of a war memento. Despite its quick demise, the Sykes-Fairbairn still had many features found in all good fighting knives. It had a double guard to protect the hand and a tapered, double-edged blade that could be honed to a razor's edge. The tip of the blade was in line with the handle when viewed from the side, allowing a straight thrusting blow. In spite of the romance of fighting knives, and the visions they conjure up of men facing each other in a jungle clearing, such flights of fancy belong mostly in the cinema. I do not mean to imply that men have not been killed with knives, but rather that the dirty work is usually done by professionals rather than amateurs, and from behind rather than in front; true fighting knives are usually reserved for taking out sentries, or in situations where it may be dangerous to discharge a firearm. Most expert knife users, including the Navy's SEAL teams, Special Forces "A" teams or Long Range Reconnaissance Patrols, must work behind enemy lines where their presence must remain unknown and any sudden noise might bring death. Yet even though these men are experts, they do not necessarily agree on knives; almost every man who orders a knife for his personal use has his own ideas of what a fighting knife should be, and the styles of weapons vary almost as widely as the personalities of their owners.

One knifemaker who has had much experience in the field of fighting blades is Dan Dennehy of Yuma, Arizona. Dan was a chief petty officer in the Navy and recently retired after thirty years at sea. Dan saw action in the Pacific during the Second World War at Saipan, Iwo Jima, Tinian and the Gilbert and Marshall Islands and began crafting fighting knives aboard ship as a hobby. Marines would hang about his metalworking shop and describe what they wanted in an ideal knife. Those early blades were usually made from old files. Dan has said if you know how to temper and control steel you can make excellent knives from files. In fact he still receives glowing letters about those old knives. During our jungle warfare in Southeast Asia, Dennehy made knives for many troops who paid their own hard-earned cash to supplement their equipment.

For close-in work, there is nothing better than a double-edged dagger, and Dennehy's close association with men involved in silent killing bears that out. It's a sad commentary on our factory products that most soldiers put their issue knives in their footlockers and ordered custom knives. One such order still makes Dennehy shudder to think about. As he describes it, "The writer went into great detail to explain the function of each part of the knife. The triangular

Overleaf: A collection of boot knives from the finest makers. Left to right: Morseth special boot model with brass-wrapped tang and ivory handle; Jess Horn tiny stag-handled model with 3¾-inch blade; Lou Booth walnut-handled model; Bob Loveless concept considered by many to be the ultimate in boot knives; George Herron model with ivory Micarta handle; Lloyd Hale knife with full tang and rosewood handle; Frank Centofante full-tang model with cocobolo handle slabs; Randall small boot knife; Jimmy Lile double-edged full-tang model with ivory handle; Ralph Bone knife with a fuller forged into the blade (it comes with a sheath of rosewood); John N. Cooper knife; Bob Dozier model with ivory slabs; Hibben knife with wood Micarta handle; Bucker Gascon knife with mesquite slabs; and John Smith double-edged narrow-tang knife with Micarta handle.

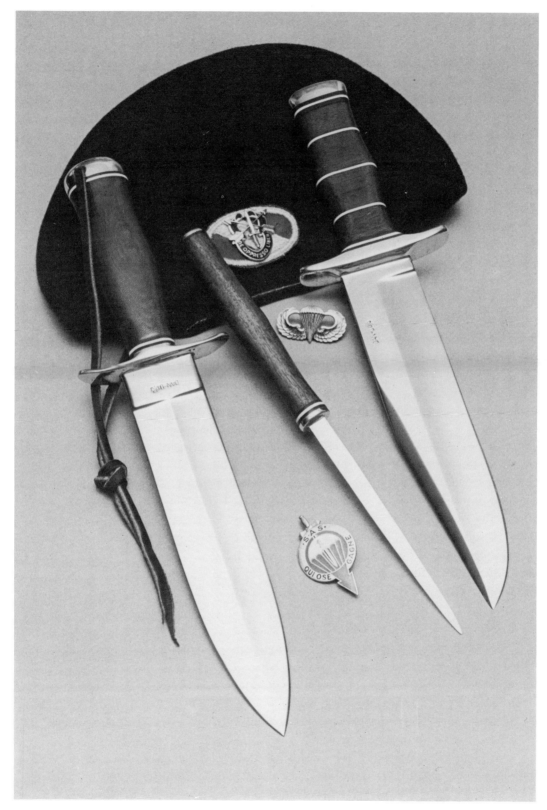

Dan Dennehy's famous fighters. Left to right, the Recon Special; Dennehy's famous triangular-bladed boot knife converted for civilian or police use; and the Green Beret.

blade was four and a half inches long with a top spike protruding from the butt about one and a half inches. The pyramid spike was to be used for temple blows, the sharpened tip and edges for throat cuts and the slim blade for shoving through the nostrils or into the ear to penetrate the brain." This gruesome weapon was crafted for a specialist assigned to deep penetration of enemy territory with the task of eliminating certain political leaders.

The butt spike is gone, but a trimmed-down version of Dennehy's combat knife is now popular with police officers and undercover narcotics agents in the Yuma area, as well as members of the sheriff's department and the Arizona Highway Patrol. The knife is light, has a round wooden handle and makes an extremely efficient weapon. Dan refuses to make one for strangers and restricts its sale to police or military.

One of Dennehy's most popular combat knives was the aptly named Recon Special, in essence a smaller version of the Roman short sword. (The original Roman blade was about eighteen inches in length and Dan's modified version runs about eight inches.) Another model that gained a great reputation with servicemen was the Green Beret. Designed by a Special Forces officer with modifications by Dennehy, it resembled a small Bowie with a blade one and a half inches wide and eight inches long. The blade top had a straight cutting edge, as opposed to the clipped edge of the original. The knife also had a double hilt and finger grooves (which Dan dislikes) and a wrist thong.

Aside from the military there are not many skilled knife fighters around these days. About twenty years ago John Styers did a fine book called *Cold Steel* published by the Marine Corps Press. It wasn't a big book, but it contained the finest explanation of knife fighting I've ever seen. Styers was a Marine who became a student of the late Colonel A. J. Drexel Biddle, dean of the close combat school, and realized the value of individual training to instill confidence in fighting men. Styers' determination and his enthusiasm for the subject eventually led to a course he conducted at various Marine, Air Force and Army bases around the country. Styers' theory was based on the age-old science of swordsmanship and used the saber fighter's stance as the foundation of the knife fighter's stance. All thrusts, attacks or defense were made from this stance, and Styers said, "The thrust, when properly executed, with your opponent within range, will be so swift he'll never see it." Styers' book has been out of print many years, but if you can locate a copy, buy it.

A good fighting knife should be about six to eight inches long and have a double edge with the point in line with the handle. Micarta would be an excellent choice for the grip. It should also have a double guard of brass or stainless steel for protection against thrusts and to catch your opponent's blade. Many of the larger blades, although popular with the military, aren't really practical in combat situations; they were ordered by people who were going into the killing business for the first time and didn't realize what was required.

Randall's famous Model 1 is a fine example of an all-purpose fighting knife. Introduced in the Second World War, it comes in three blade lengths, six, seven, and eight inches, with the false edge sharpened approximately three inches. It may be had with a Commando-style handle in line with the point at no extra charge.

A trio of solid fighting knives. At top is a fighter by Bucker Gascon with 6-inch blade and Texas mesquite slab handle. In this instance the wood is cut against the grain, giving an unusual effect. Center model is by Bill Sonneville with ivory Micarta handle. At bottom is John Smith's sleek fighter, the Model #5, in light Micarta with brass trim and butt.

At top, Bo Randall's famous Model 1, probably the most copied fighting knife in history. It is available with 6-, 7- and 8-inch blade. It was widely used by Allied troops in World War II, and has been used in every theater of war ever since. The unusual center knife is the Weatherford Brothers Shark Fighter with damascened blade and ivory Micarta handle slabs. At bottom is a specially designed fighter by John Nelson Cooper.

Full-sized fighters. From left to right: Morseth lugged-hilt model with Micarta handle; Bob Loveless full-tang fighter with Micarta slabs; Lloyd Hale fighter, a companion to his boot knife; John Nelson Cooper model with leather-wrapped handle; and George Stone fighter with butt cap of nickel silver.

From left to right: Bucker Gascon model with cocobolo slabs; one of Ed Henry's famous fighters with nonslip grip; a small knife by Jim Mustin of Cajun Knives, with ebony handle; George Herron fighter with stag handle; and Ralph Bone Model B, fashioned after the British Commando knife.

Boot knives, so called from the days when many a man carried a knife concealed in his boot, are really small fighting knives with a compromise. Because they must be kept to a concealable size, the handles must be small, the crossguard either short or nonexistent, and the blade short as well. A small handle does not offer a secure enough grip for dueling, a missing crossguard can cost you a thumb, and a four-inch blade against a seven-inch means three inches of reach that could prove fatal. Yet boot knives are stealthy little buggers, and make a fine backup weapon. Consider the police officer's armament, for instance. His official duty weapon may be a Smith & Wesson or Colt .38 caliber, and this is the gun he uses in trouble. Still, many law enforcement officers carry a .22 caliber Derringer hidden in a handcuff case, or elsewhere on their person. No policeman intends to get into a gun fight with a .22; it's a backup weapon to save his life in a tight situation. Boot knives serve the same purpose.

One of the slickest boot knives on the market is that made by Morseth Knives. It's well thought out and beautifully crafted from an excellent design. The blade is four inches long and can be sharpened on both sides if desired. The handle is black Micarta, although a deluxe model with ivory handle and brass-wrapped tang is also available. The handle design permits an exceptionally comfortable grip and flattens out near the guard for placement of thumb and forefinger for thrusting. The sheath is backed with Velcro and another strip may be sewn or glued inside the boot or along the flat of a belt. One of the trickier aspects of these small blades is their lightness, and they may be hidden many places about the person.

Bob Loveless has given much thought to fighting and boot knives, and has a winner with his five-inch boot knife. Loveless says flatly that his fighting knives are not all-purpose knives. They are made to be used as weapons, meant for killing, and he offers no apologies for making them. One day the world may be full of love and respect for all men; it isn't that way now and such knives are still needed by a few men in out-of-the-way places. Loveless' boot knife is a trim, very nasty-looking fellow with a typical Loveless handle and a slight drop point, although the tip does remain in line with the handle. Loveless has sold many of these deadly blades to members of the F.B.I. and agents of the C.I.A. Bob's fighting knives and a small four-and-a-half-inch Hide-Out Knife complement the boot knife. His fighters follow the same general outline, but run a bit longer, six and a half inches.

Many knifesmiths who craft this type of knife emulate other work, but John Smith and Jess Horn have both created fine boot knives of original design. The Smith version is about five inches long and has black Micarta handles and a dagger-shaped blade with both edges sharpened. Jess Horn's tiny blade is only three and three-quarters inches long and spear-shaped, with a full-tang handle only three inches long that fits the palm of your hand. The sheath for this small knife has a metal clip attached that slips onto your boot or belt. Tie thongs can also be used for fastening on parts of your clothing. This is a slight but deadly knife.

Survival knives are completely different in function. Basically, they are something *you have with you* when you encounter a survival situation. Hence the single greatest criticism of most "survival" knives is that they are too long and heavy; many are the size of short swords, and are likely to be left behind when they are needed most. Survival knives from the more realistic makers run to seven or eight inches at most, and are not a burden to carry hour after hour, day in and day out. A good survival knife should be light enough to wear at all times and never intrude. To that we might add it should also be fairly compact and as comfortable to wear as a piece of clothing. If a knife is light and comfortable, you invariably have it along when needed. And any knife, if you have it with you, is better than the finest specialized tool if you don't.

Many survival knives carry the appellation "combat-survival." I suppose that's all right if you want to dramatize a situation, but whatever you call them, they're small, handy knives to have along when you get into trouble. And though any good knife can be a survival tool, knives specially crafted for the purpose have a couple of extra gadgets that might come in handy. The double hilt usually has a couple of holes drilled on each side for fastening to a pole since a spear is sometimes much more practical. Knives of this type usually have a row of sawteeth atop the blade as an aid in cutting out of downed aircraft, though it's a moot point if they'd do much good against plexiglass. Many models have hollow handles secured with a leakproof O ring, rendering the interior waterproof.

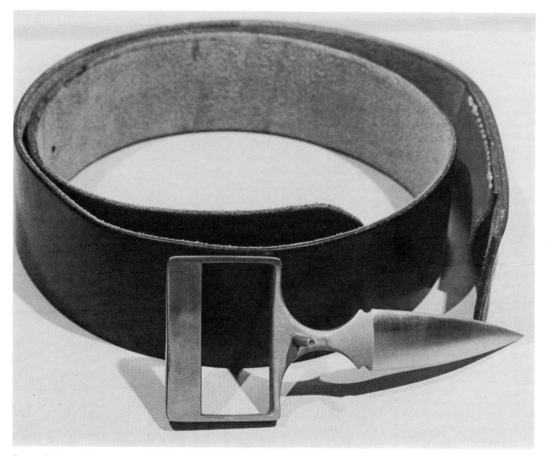

One of the oddest knives to come along in years and the hit of the 1972 Kansas City show—Blackie Collins Survivor Belt, a double-edged dagger worn as a belt buckle. Note the small sheath for the blade on the inner belt.

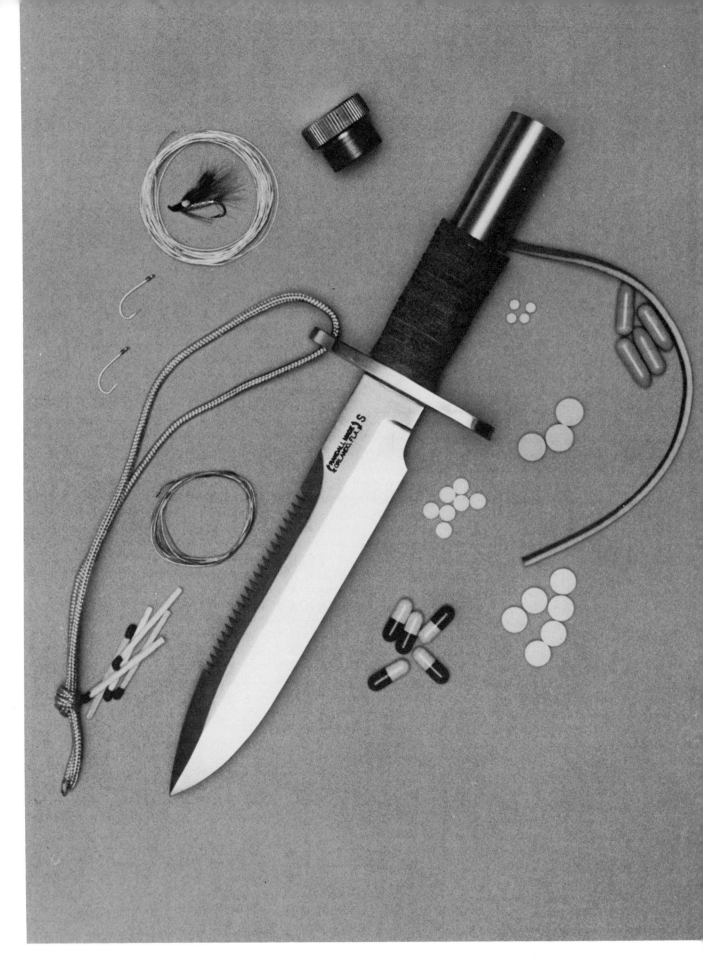

Randall's Model 18 is a combat-survival knife that was designed for Captain George Ingraham of the 94th Medical Detachment while on duty in Vietnam. The knife is actually an improved version of the Model 14 with sawteeth added, plus a hollow stainless-steel handle. Captain Ingraham reported that the saw edge could easily cut through the skin of a downed chopper, and any sportsman could easily adapt the handle for his particular needs. Ingraham made a good case for an all-round survival outfit by wrapping the handle with a layer of monofiliment to be used as fish line. Over this went a guitar string for small game snares, and the whole thing was covered with two leather bootlaces. Into the handle went water purification tablets, Dexedrine, codeine pills, morphine, anti-malaria tablets, fishhooks, extra line and waterproof matches. The whole affair made a neat and compact piece of survival gear, and the five-and-a-half-inch blade wouldn't be too big to wear all day.

Any of these knives will serve you well, but before you think about toting a fighting or boot knife, remember that they are classified as weapons in most parts of the country. To be caught with one might mean trouble, and it's almost guaranteed to get you bounced off any commercial airline. Don't say you weren't warned. Still, if you feel you want a fighting knife, by all means order one. They are fascinating weapons and will add interest to any knife collection, even if they never draw blood.

Opposite: Randall's Model 18 Attack-Survival knife with equipment that fits into the handle. The knife is surrounded by fishhooks, fishline, snares and strangling wires, waterproof matches, morphine tablets, pep pills for escape and evasion, water purification tablets and antibiotics for wounds or infection. Handle is wound with rawhide thong for aid in fastening knife to pole for use as a spear. O-ring keeps the handle compartment completely waterproof.

chapter 6

folding knives

Of all the knives carried by man these days, the ordinary pocketknife is undoubtedly the most popular. This hasn't always been the case, but the pocketknife goes back a long way in history. Specimens have been found in Roman ruins, and an early seventeenth-century model found at Jamestown reposes in our National Museum. They've been called everything from clasp knives to pocketknives to jackknives to penknives, and while some of these were general terms used to describe a small folder, many did refer to specific designs. The small penknife, for example, was a necessary aid in trimming turkey-quill pens in olden times long before the advent of the steel nib. By whatever name, pocketknives have long been the boon companions of most men who grew up far from our sprawling cities and the most cherished possession of generations of small boys.

Early jackknives were fairly large two-bladed affairs, and over the years the basic mechanism has changed very little. However, the blade and design variations of folders are almost infinite. During the Second World War the Office of Strategic Services even had a well-known firm make a pocketknife with various tools for picking locks!

Modern cutlery firms turn out a staggering number of pocketknives in any given week, one outfit alone claiming an average weekly run of ten thousand dozen of just one model.

With so many modestly priced folders available, it might be fair to wonder why custom knifemakers bother to undertake the long and tedious business of handcrafting folding knives. As usual there are a number of reasons. First,

folders are a real challenge, and some knifemakers aren't really happy unless they're picking up a gauntlet. More important, perhaps, is the fact that there's a good market for them. Some men feel foolish with a belt knife hanging from their hip, and prefer an inconspicuous folder carried in a pocket. This even includes some experienced hunters, and they have the skill to skin a moose with a penknife. Finally, many collectors are interested in folding knives, especially those of unusual or innovative design.

Even Bill Moran, one of the most conservative knifemakers, took the plunge with a one-bladed locking folder produced in 1972. The work is so exacting that Bill only makes fifteen or twenty a year, and every one is presold. One difficulty with folders is that all springs must be made and tempered by hand and carefully fitted into the small recesses of the body of the knife. All Moran's knives are highly decorated with carved silver, and the handles of ivory or curly maple are inlaid with silver wire. Moran feels we've entered a golden age of knifemaking, with many collectors willing to pay high prices for exhibition pieces that are more works of art than working knives. Although he's had requests for a working folder, Moran says there is little reason to use an expensive folder for daily tasks and has even talked customers out of higher priced models on occasion. Bill feels the only reason for buying one of his fancy folders is the ornate decor. With prices ranging up to $400 and a wait of several years for delivery, there is some doubt if one will ever be used on a hunting trip!

Until recently most handcrafted pocketknives were one-bladed affairs, but George Stone joined Jess Horn with a two-bladed model, the Stone Trapper, crafted of stainless steel and made with the meticulous attention Stone gives all his knives. Building these folders is a new venture for Stone and the knives will be produced in limited quantity for discriminating collectors. After much consideration Stone decided not to craft a lock-open style of folder, as do many makers, but constructed a traditional folding knife that really is small enough to fit your pocket. The side plates, bolsters and rivets are of type 303 stainless steel with back springs of a rust-resistant spring steel buffed to a high polish. Internal plates are engine-turned and the handle slabs are of Micarta, stag or ivory, all dovetailed and held with epoxy, rivets and a center through pin. Stone's folders are as sturdy as his name and should last through many hunts.

In Ron Lake's case, most of the ideas for his famous folder were derived from thinking of what he wanted in a personal knife while avoiding what he considered bad points in production knives. It all began when a friend brought him one of the better-known commercial folders to be repaired. While repairing the knife Ron could see obvious weak points, and he decided to improve on them with his own knife. For example, he wanted a knife that would be easy to open and accordingly fitted a hardened steel bushing at the pivot point. He also cut a nail nick for either hand and the knife may be opened by simply pushing the blade out with one hand while holding the knife in working position.

The idea of inlaying the handle material into the frame had been in the back

Overleaf: Folders can be classical or innovative. The upper knife is a replica Remington Bullet Knife by Blackie Collins. It is a two-bladed knife with Delrin handles and was authorized by the Remington Arms Company. The bottom knife is a Bob Ogg folder with rosewood handles and fine acid etching by Shaw-Leibowitz.

96

Bill Moran "art" knives. These handsome blades have carved nickel-silver bolsters. The wood-handled model is of maple inlaid with silver wire. The others have ivory handles.

of his head for some time, and the repair job, with covers (slabs) cracked and chipped along the edges, reminded him of it. The handle material in Lake's design is protected by the frame, which is machined from a solid piece of metal and recessed for the slabs. This treatment protects the edges and gives strength to such fragile materials as ivory and ebony.

Perhaps the most unusual feature of the Lake knife is its locking release tab. Where other makers place this atop the handle, Lake uses a long lever with a stainless-steel tab at the end. Wisely locating this tab at the very end of the handle, Lake ensures a smooth line and simplifies cleaning this sensitive area. After use you simply pull a cloth under the tab. Lake's knife is not small, although it would be unfair to say it couldn't be carried in the pocket. To dispel any arguments on this score Andy Russell has convinced Ron a smaller, slimmer model should be constructed following the same general outlines and methods of construction. This new knife, known as the Lake-Russell folder, is available direct from Russell Knives if you're willing to part with a little more than $125.

Few handmade folders are inexpensive; most run double or triple the price of a modest sheath knife. Even so, Bob Ogg sticks exclusively with folding knives and makes it pay without charging an arm and a leg. Ogg had been making sheath knives as a hobby for years when a man walked into his shop one day and asked if he'd repair a knife. "I agree," relates Bob, "and the guy

A selection of fine handcrafted folders. Top row from left: Jess Horn Remington Bullet Knife with stag handle; two Bob Ogg knives, one with stag and the other with Osage-orange grips; another Horn California bolster knife; Henry Frank engraved model; and unusual Ted Dowell folder with Micarta slabs. Bottom row from left: two folders by Ron Lake of stainless steel inlaid with cocobolo; another Lake model, a slimmer style designed by Andy Russell and made exclusively for him by Lake; large knife by Ralph Bone with rosewood handle and brass bolsters; and twin-bladed model, the Trapper, by George Stone.

trots out an old folder with a broken spring. It was a challenge, but I made him a new spring and put it together. Simple! So I thought, why not try starting from scratch and see what I could do? Not so simple!"

Now after making folders for a number of years Ogg considers the fixed-blade knife as child's play and boring to make. With more than 300 folders to his credit, Bob makes nothing else. Bob's main objective is to construct a plain, simple, rugged handmade knife at a reasonable price. Even with extra cost refinements you can load your Ogg knife with goodies and be hard put to spend over $50.

Ogg's standard blade steel is C-1095, which tests out between Rockwell 54 and 58. Blades run from one-eighth to one-sixteenth inch in thickness, and bolsters are solid brass. On special order Bob will use O-1 tool steel, but feels it's not really a lot better than C-1095. It usually takes from six to ten hours of work to make a fine folder, and Bob has abandoned construction of locking-action knives, feeling that they are much more complicated to produce. Bob bluntly said, "I feel anyone who is afraid of using a knife without a safety lock just doesn't know how to use a knife and has no business owning one." For handle material Bob opts for Micarta, giving it full marks for durability. Of the other materials he feels stag makes a pretty handle, but admits it often ends up thicker than he prefers, since he is always hesitant about grinding off too much material. Ivory, buffalo horn and ebony are all beautiful but unstable and Bob prefers not using them unless the customer insists. Although Ogg makes only six models there are considerable possibilities for variation, mixing handle and blade shapes and varying the size and proportion. Added to that, any of his knives may be built in magnum or mini versions, and if you have your own idea of what a folding knife should be, Ogg is delighted to see your sketch. In fact, he has a standing offer of a free knife for any new idea that leads to a model for his line.

The one man who has come up with the most innovative recent idea in folding knives isn't a knifemaker at all, but a designer, engineer and oceanographer named Barry Wood. We all think we get great ideas from time to time, but most of us lack the tools or talent to carry them out. When Wood decided to build a better mousetrap his background and training supplied the know-how, and the result was a design some knife fanciers consider the first breakthrough in folding knives in over a hundred years.

The Wood knife has to be seen to be believed. The best way I can describe it is to say it swings open and closed something like a scissors. There are no springs or locks and all three pieces, blade and both handle sides, pivot on one large stainless steel pin. Since the design has no springs there is no chance for failure through breakage or metal fatigue. When Colt Firearms first saw the knife they gave Wood an order for five hundred per month to be sold under the Colt label, and Wood, with the help of family and friends, has put in many eighty-hour weeks cranking up production.

A significant feature of these knives is that the design has no hidden areas for dirt build-up to hinder opening or closing. It may be washed off under a faucet or in the nearest stream after use. Wood offers three models with handcrafted blades and Micarta handles—a general utility blade, caper and skinner.

The knives of Barry Wood. Wood's knives all have the unique scissorslike method of opening. These models have various Micarta handles.

Jimmy Lile, who likes to be called the Arkansas Knifesmith, recently introduced three fine folders. Lile, an excellent maker of sheath knives, has also become intrigued with the possibilities of folders. After a thorough job of research Lile introduced three models. One is two-bladed with various materials used for the sides. Of the other two the most unusual has steel sides of 440-C, to match the blade, and is practically an all-stainless knife.

Jess Horn is best known for his immaculate Remington Bullet Knife, which seems to have started the run on folders and now comes in three sizes. For the advanced collector, one of Horn's Bullet models is a replica of Remington's Model R 1126 and has two blades exactly like the original. The other is a copy of the famous Model R 1306. Both have blades three and a half inches long with stag handles and are crafted of carbon tool steel. Horn uses a special method of his own to prevent carbon from leaving the steel during the hardening process. Since he does all the hardening and tempering himself, rather

Henry Frank knives with magnificent engraving on blade and bolsters. All have ivory slab handles with the exception of the dark handle, which is of buffalo horn.

Four ivory-handled folders by masters of their trade. From top to bottom: Ralph Bone; Henry Frank; the Beta model designed by A. G. Russell and crafted by Bob Ogg; and another Ogg folder.

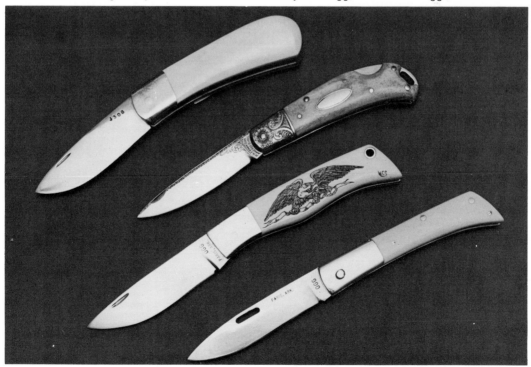

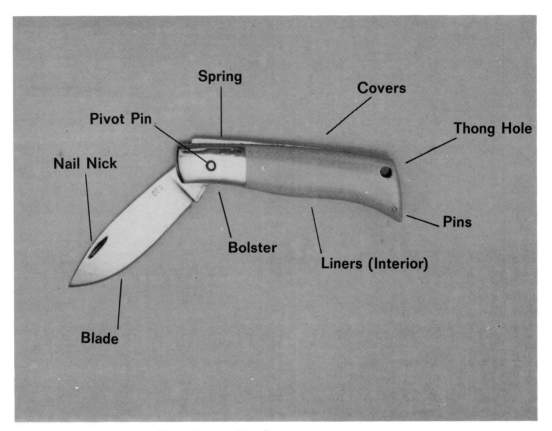

Folding-knife nomenclature. The knife is by Bob Ogg.

than sending it out for commercial treatment, Horn can exercise more than normal care and control during this delicate part of knifemaking. His latest addition is a replica Barlow knife, and he plans to extend his line since his folders have proved so popular with sportsmen. Horn has recently teamed up with Bob Loveless to offer a line of knives under the Horn/Loveless label. Crafted of 154-CM steel, these knives will have blades done by Loveless and assembly by Horn.

Atlantan Blackie Collins has also introduced a Remington Bullet Knife, Model 1123. Collins charges $100, which is in keeping with most of the prices of fine folders.

Another series of folders is produced by Ralph Bone with ivory, stag or Micarta handles. Bone was originally a partner of George Stone; they went their separate ways a number of years ago and each continues to do fine work. The Bone folders are handsome knives, and the Model J will do most any outdoor job. It has a four-inch blade and comes with either rosewood or ivory handle. The other Bone model is slightly smaller and can also be had with a variety of handle material.

Even Bucker Gascon has gotten into the act of crafting a folder. He has come up with an unusually attractive drop-point model with Osage-orange handle. Gascon's first folder model is certainly a winner in design. The blade is slightly over three inches of 440-C and the unique handle is handsome with various hues of yellow and orange.

Ted Dowell admits his $200 folder hunter is a little expensive. And so he has introduced a less expensive model at a quarter the price that combines the features of a slim practical folder and might let you win money at the bar when your buddies try figuring out how it works. Somewhat derivative of a Philippine folder, the protective guard must be swung back, then moved into the handle, swinging out the blade at the same time. This knife has a blade of the new D-2 steel and Micarta handle.

The Las Vegas show of 1970 was obviously memorable for Loveless since he ran across a magnificently engraved locked-blade folder crafted by Henry Frank. Frank can both build a fine knife and engrave it in the European tradition. Frank was a relative unknown at the time, but it was decided he should offer his work through the Loveless shop, and this superlative maker quietly earned recognition as one of the finest craftsmen making knives today. His engraving ranks with the best found on quality guns, making his knives true works of art, or "instant heirlooms," as they have been called. Aside from their beauty and high quality they are strongly made and intended for serious use. Frank works with AISI Grade O-7 tool steel, which makes a high-quality blade that holds up well in service, and other parts of the knife have the finest materials including main springs, locking bar, bolsters and scales. Frank's knives are offered in two grades, the Plain Grade, with a few simple and tasteful adornments, and the Engraved Grade, which is fully hand-engraved on both sides of the blade, with bolsters hand-cut in keeping with blade design. Bolsters are nickel silver or gold with stainless-steel liners, and handle slabs are usually tusk ivory. Mr. Frank's prizes aren't cheap.

Folding knives have attracted specialist collectors, and some men have fine collections already. The modern folder is so new, and many design concepts are so original that they represent a tremendous improvement over what has been seen in the past. Folders have found a home with modern knifesmiths and are definitely here to stay.

chapter 7

the Bowie

Amateur historians are sometimes more romantic than novelists and often produce about the same mixture of fact and fiction. With their help, the story of the Bowie knife has gradually been transformed from an actual happening to a fairy tale for grownups. By now the truths and half-truths have so run together, like quicksilver, that there is no longer any clear dividing line between fact and fiction. There is no objection to calling the Bowie the most famous (or infamous, if you prefer) knife in American history, but the tales surrounding the blade and its originator have long since become confusing enough to confound the most ardent mystery fan.

Of this much we are certain: There was indeed a Colonel James Bowie, a real figure of history who loomed larger than life even in his own time. Bowie was known for carrying a big blade, but if he ever carried a knife made by one James Black, or even if Black ever existed, is open for conjecture. Certainly many historians wonder if there ever was a James Black, or if he were indeed a figment of someone's imagination. Black was supposed to be a fine cutler, yet no one then or now seems ever to have seen a Bowie, or for that matter any other knife, crafted by this faceless man. What could have become of all those fine blades crafted by this legendary wonder? Certainly any man with pride in his craft would have marked his work in some way, but while we can still find Bowies made by other English and American knifesmiths, not one Black Bowie has appeared.

There is also doubt as to the date when the knife was supposedly made. Some say 1830 and others pin it down precisely to November 1831. You can find plenty of proponents on both sides to back their particular point of view

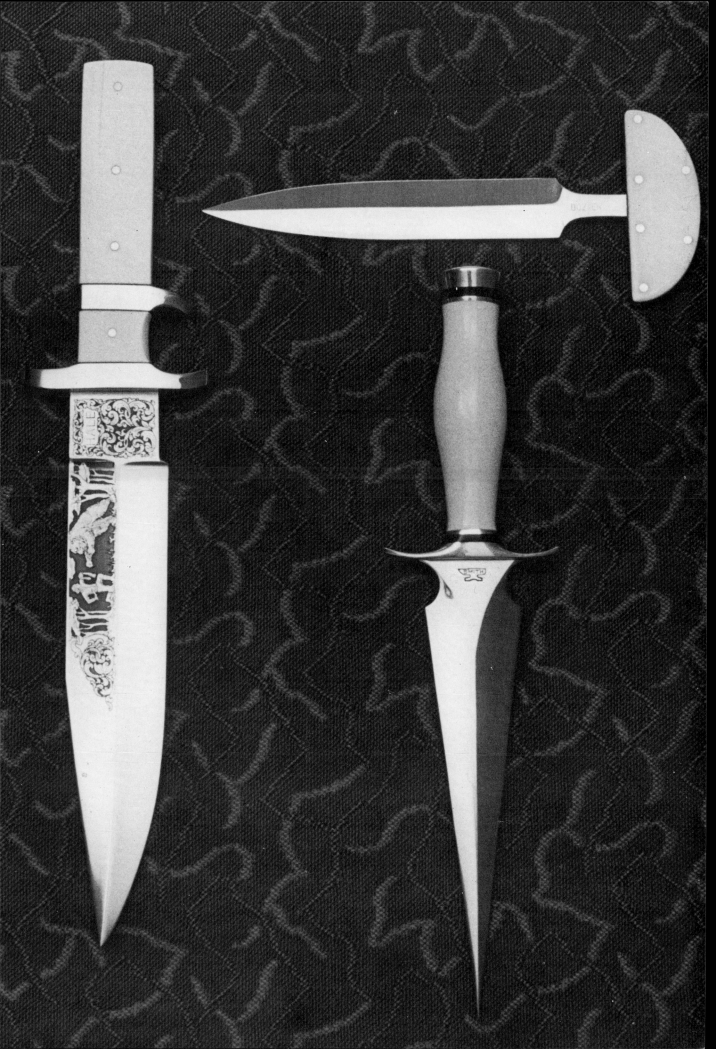

and there are enough historical data to prove both arguments at the same time.

In a way it's a pity, because the Bowie knife is a famous part of American history, like, say, the Kentucky rifle and the early Winchesters and Colts. Yet all these bits of historical memorabilia can be traced, documented and dated—all, that is, but the Bowie. In any event, no Bowie knife known to have been carried by the Colonel or made by Black is in existence. We might add a question mark even to this statement because rumors have persisted over the years that an original Black Bowie reposes in a mysterious bank vault somewhere in Arkansas. Yet if this is true the family that owns this blade has never shown it to any expert for authentication, nor will they come forth to prove or disprove the story itself.

The brief story of the Bowie, if you don't know it, goes something like this: James Bowie's older brother, Rezin, an enthusiastic hunter of game in Louisiana and Mississippi, had a knife made purely for hunting. It was a simple knife, and nothing would have brought it to the attention of history had not Rezin given it to James to protect himself from a certain Major Wright who had shot at him while unarmed in the course of an argument. Shortly after receiving the knife Bowie put it to use on his assailant at the famous Vidalia Sandbar fight. Though shot in the hip and stabbed by a sword cane, he managed to dispatch Major Wright, wound another assailant and survive.

The Wright affair was typical of the era and the details are of some interest. Major Norris Wright wasn't altogether a bad sort, though he had a bit of the scoundrel in him. But perhaps he wore too many hats—bank officer, respected merchant and sheriff of Rapides Parish in Louisiana. While wearing his bank director fedora one day Wright turned down Bowie's request for a loan, thereby incurring his wrath. They met on the street soon afterwards. An argument started which soon degenerated into a tirade of insults. Bowie upbraided the Major unmercifully and gave him a veritable tongue lashing. A crowd gathered, much to the embarrassment of Wright, and his fury at Bowie mounted until he could contain himself no longer. Lashed beyond all reason, Wright drew his pistol and fired point-blank at Bowie. Unfortunately for Wright, he committed the grave error of not killing his enemy. The ball, depending upon which version of history you read, (1) was deflected by a twig or branch; (2) hit a watch in Bowie's pocket; (3) hit Bowie and caused a furrow to rip across his chest. Whatever did happen, Bowie (1) grabbed his gun, or (2) being unarmed was given a gun by someone in the crowd and the damned thing misfired. Bowie, by now in a rage himself, rushed at Wright with swinging fists, only to be restrained by onlookers.

Soon after this encounter Bowie began carrying his brother Rezin's hunting knife in the obvious belief that a working blade would be more reliable than a nonworking gun. It was this weapon, with its reputed strong guard and blade, nine and a quarter inches long, that appears to have been the first Bowie to draw blood in combat.

Bowie was not, as history might have you believe, a Galahad in armor nor a man schooled in the fine art of being a gentleman. Frank D. Praytor in his

Overleaf: Three ivory-handled knives of the Bowie type. The Bowie with sub-hilt is by Lloyd Hale, a full-tang knife with ivory slabs and etching by Shaw-Leibowitz. Push dagger with halfmoon handle is by Bob Dozier. The small Arkansas toothpick is by John Smith.

excellent treatise *Knife Fighter* refers to Bowie as "a slave trader, smuggler, confidence man and forger although at the Alamo on 6 March, 1836 he fought and died with bravery perhaps balancing the ledger on a less than virtuous life." Well, he didn't even do that, but we get ahead of our story. Out of the sandbar battle came Bowie, although sorely wounded and hanging onto life by less than a couple of threads, with a reputation as a supreme knife fighter and fame as a hero. In fact, the style of fighting used by Bowie would set the standards for knife combat in years to come. While Rezin's knife drew first blood it also opened the way for a national fad and years of ensuing terror when everyone—farmers, gamblers, private citizens, knaves and congressmen alike—carried the swordlike blade.

In 1830 or the fall of 1831 (history is hazy on this point) Bowie and a certain James Black supposedly met and created the devil's own weapon. Black, a transplanted citizen of New Jersey, was then residing in Washington, Arkansas, a crude frontier village. Black had set himself up as a blacksmith, and thanks to his early apprenticeship as a silver plater in Philadelphia, he could plate knives and offer something fancier than the crude run of craftsmanship. Black soon became so popular he found himself making blades to the exclusion of all other work. His fame as a cutler spread far, and the demand for his knives, tempered better than anything of that period, soon gave him all the work he could handle.

The Black legend has it that he possessed the secret of Damascus blades, but if that is so, his methods of tempering died with him. In later years, it is said, Black often remarked that there were twelve processes through which he put his knives. However, as he grew older he was unable to recall even one, and the legacy of steel which he hoped to pass on to those who were kind to him died with his passing.

A former governor of Arkansas, Daniel W. Jones, the son of the late Dr. Isaac N. Jones in whose home Black, then old and blind, spent his remaining years, wrote that Black, trying to recall his technique and write it down, spent hours of anguish alone in a room and finally cried out, "My God! My God! It has all gone from me." But all this came later, for when Black met Bowie they were both stout young men. In view of Black's growing reputation as a cutler, it was small wonder that Bowie made a beeline for his smithy when he arrived in town. Bowie wanted a knife within two or three months and left a sketch for its manufacture.

Prices for a knife from Black's forge ranged widely from $5 to $50, no doubt reflecting the amount of gold or silver covering the knife. Each knife on completion was tested on an old hickory axe handle for half an hour. If the knife wouldn't shave the hair off your arm after this treatment it was tossed away. Yet with all that has been recorded little is known of Bowie's design and less of Black's contribution or the fee charged by Black for his services.

Black, as the story goes, supposedly made two knives, one following Bowie's design and another of his own creation. When Bowie returned he hefted both knives and stated a preference for Black's innovation. The new knife was a frightening weapon to behold, though its actual length is unknown. (It apparently grew each time it was unsheathed.) From the standpoint of utility most authorities believe it was probably around twelve inches in length, al-

Top to bottom: fine Lloyd Hale Bowie with rosewood handle and nickel-silver butt; Ed Henry Bowie with stag slab handle; and Corbet Sigman Bowie with cocobolo handle and nickel-silver butt in the English style.

HALE

HENRY

C.R. SIGMAN
RED HOUSE, W.VA.

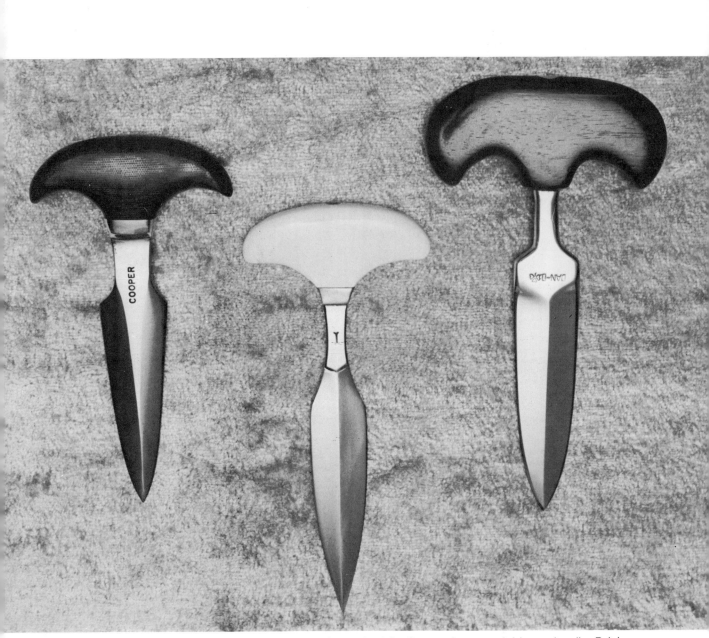

Three variations of the push dagger. From left to right: John Cooper dagger with Micarta handle; Ralph Bone dagger with ivory handle; Dan Dennehy dagger with large ebony handle.

though some experts argue for a blade as long as fourteen to sixteen inches. The width was probably one and three-quarters inches and the bottom, which was sharpened, ran straight from the heel for roughly one third its length and then curved gently upward toward the tip. The top edge dipped in a concave curve and was razor-sharp. Bowie's new knife, his skill with it and his apparent eagerness to demonstrate that skill, made both him and his creation famous overnight. He did not necessarily revolutionize the ancient art of knife fighting, but he demonstrated the potential of the weapon for a whole new generation.

The Black Bowie, while regarded as the ultimate refinement of brother Rezin's hunting blade, was probably preceded by another knife turned out by an unknown blacksmith named Snowden. It is a fact that Bowie had a duel with a well-known gambler named Sturdivant in 1829, shortly before Black entered the picture, and some historians regard this knife as the evolutionary link between Rezin's blades and Black's triumph. Whatever the connection, Black's prowess as the historically accepted innovator of the Bowie gained him fame and orders to "make me a knife like Jim Bowie's" soon became "make me a Bowie knife."

Before Black became old, ill and blind in his last years, he must have made hundreds of knives like the Bowie, yet not one of these fine steel blades has ever been found that can be directly attributed to Black's own hand, which certainly seems passing strange. For though they are not exactly plentiful, there are enough Bowies in public and private collections to enable any student to study and examine them at leisure. William R. Williamson, the noted Santa Barbara, California, collector and authority on Bowies, doubts very much that Bowie and Black ever met, and feels Black was a figment of Governor Jones' fertile imagination. Williamson has taken a different tack, and in tracing blade styles has found the Bowie type of knife in existence at least a hundred years before Bowie's time in history. For that matter, other famed craftsmen like Michael Price of San Francisco admittedly did make Bowie-type knives.

However, the big trend to Bowies came only when the English trade got wind of the knife's popularity, and the factories of Sheffield and Birmingham began directing the bulk of their output to the American market. Sheffield's Washington Works sent a representative to America in 1830 and he soon got the equivalent of tennis elbow writing orders for Bowie knives. At that time the knife was so popular that anyone venturing out of doors seems to have felt naked without one tucked into his belt.

Important cities from New Orleans to St. Louis had knife-fighting schools—study under professionals was advisable if you carried a knife and wanted to survive a reasonable number of your allotted three score and ten. Huge knives such as the Bowie (and any large knife with double guard and a sharpened clip point was called a Bowie) were impractical as hunting or skinning knives, yet crafters of Bowies swarmed west and brought the Bowie onto the plains in the 1870s. As the Bowie headed west, its most terrible days were still seen in those cities hugging the great rivers. Murders and duels were committed with the Bowie with such frequency that many states began to ban the knife. Alabama enacted a law in 1837, but Mississippi beat its neighbor by two weeks with "An Act to Prevent the Evil Practice of Duelling in This State and for Other Purposes." In various sections of the law, weapons were clearly defined: rifle, shotgun, sword, pistol *and Bowie knife.* The following year saw the Tennessee legislature pass the most stringent and far-reaching anti-Bowie law of all. It was called "An Act to Suppress the Sale and Use of Bowie Knives and Arkansas Tooth-Picks in This State," and ran into five well-defined sections spelling out precisely who could or could not sell, carry or possess the knife, in the manner of modern handgun and firearms control laws. (The Arkansas toothpick was a rather slim knife derived from the naval dirk.)

Bowies were not solely responsible for the untimely deaths of the period. Another knife that appeared around 1848 was the push dagger. It was a fairly small, reasonably concealable weapon and much favored by gamblers, card sharps and other gentlemen of the sporting fraternity. In fact it made a death-dealing weapon of no mean purpose. The grip of the dagger was in the shape of a T bar across the top and rested in the palm, making it an excellent thrusting tool. One blow was usually sufficient to put your opponent *hors de combat*—if it wasn't it was wise to retire because a derringer might blow a hole in your stomach. And there were other lethal knives—but it is the Bowie we remember.

If little is known of the Bowie's origin even less is recorded of its end, and what really became of the original Bowie knife will probably never be known. Some tales say it was tossed on Bowie's funeral pyre at the Alamo and others have it toted off to Mexico by some unknown soldier. Bowie died an ignominious death during the final throes of the Alamo, lying wasted on his bed, prostrated by consumption, pneumonia, or both. The final scene depicted by some historians of Bowie swiping at the swarming Mexicans with knife in hand simply defies logic.

Whatever the true facts of the Jim Bowie legend it's an intriguing story, and it's not surprising that the Bowie knife, although clouded in the darkness of the past, has captured the imagination of many collectors and knifemakers. Almost every custom cutler at one time or another tries his hand at crafting a Bowie. His interpretation of the original knife will seldom stray too far afield of what is generally accepted. Blade length may vary according to the whim of the maker or desire of the collector, but it will still be a Bowie. Certain embellishments of engraving on the blade, ivory grips, or gold and silver inlay may fancy it up, but it will still be a Bowie.

A handsome presentation piece by Jess Horn of Redding, Calif. The magnificent English-style Bowie has a rosewood-and-silver handle, and the handmade sheath is trimmed with silver.

Of all the modern knifemakers in our country today the acknowledged master of the Bowie is D. E. Henry of Mountain Ranch, California. To say Henry makes a pretty good Bowie is like saying that Enzo Ferrari builds a pretty good motor car. They are both masters in fields in which it takes an extra touch of class to raise you above the crowd. Happily, you can buy one of Mr. Henry's masterpieces for somewhat less than one of Mr. Ferrari's.

Henry's Bowies are famed for their impeccable workmanship and attention to detail. The blades are hand-polished which means what it says—no power tools or buffing machines are used as substitutes for long tedious hours of muscle power. Henry figures he works about five hours per inch of blade, and his ten-inch Bowie will run you about $300. A choice of ivory or stag for the handle slabs will cost extra, as will a reinforced silver guard. You might also toss in another $40 or so for a handsome silver-mounted scabbard. If these prices seem steep, bear in mind that they work out to about $6 per hour, which is modest enough for the work of a superior craftsman. Henry's Bowies, like his other knives, are collector's items traded among connoisseurs with the value increasing each time.

Before he became interested in knives, back in 1948, Henry was personnel manager of an electronics plant in California. He decided to get out of the rush of city life and head for the peace and quiet of the countryside. Of all his knives, the Bowie is obviously his first love. Like most quality knifemakers Henry has a backlog of orders most times, and customers may be assured of a minimum wait of at least two years for one of his beauties, but if you fancy the Bowie, D. E. Henry's blades are worth the wait.

A new knifemaker, Lloyd Hale, is rapidly becoming famed for his Bowies, and rightly so. For a year or so Hale was resident knifesmith at Black's Forge in Washington, Arkansas, crafting knives at a replica of Black's original smithy. Hale has said, "Custom knifemaking is an art through which each craftsman expresses himself as an individual." Hale's interpretation of the Bowie is as fine and artful as any made today, and points to the growing ability of a man who has been making knives only a short time. Hale's Bowies are made by the stock-removal method from O-1 oil-hardened tool steel, although he will obtain and use any steel the customer desires. A production machinist before becoming a full-time knifemaker, Hale does meticulous work.

Another new maker who seems to have recently discovered the Bowie is Corbet Sigman. For some time, bigger knives held no particular fascination for Sigman and he had no use for the Bowie either as a practical tool or as a decoration. However, with his growing clientele among quality-conscious collectors Sigman was soon asked to make one. With the first model underway Sigman found to his delight that he enjoyed working with larger pieces of steel for a change. Now he finds a growing fascination with the knife, though he has not added the Bowie to his line.

The oldest maker of fine Bowies—seventy-some years—is Rudy Ruana of Bonner, Montana. Ruana's knives, including the Bowies, are among the biggest bargains around, with prices for the finest running comfortably under $100. Rudy has led a colorful life, starting as a private in the Third Field Artillery with the duties of blacksmith. He made his first knife when two Indian horse-skinners, unhappy with their issue blades that dulled too quickly, asked the

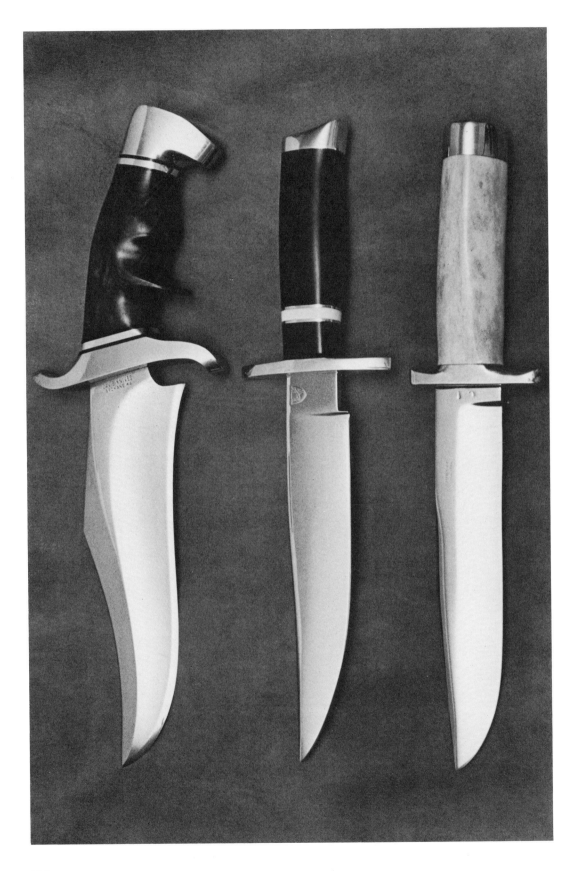

young smithy to craft a knife that would work. Taking a leaf spring from an old Ford, Ruana fashioned a sturdy knife and his Indian friends went away happy. Since those days Ruana has been a farmer, worked in a garage and spent time with the Forest Service. During the Second World War the demand for knives kept him busy, but Rudy returned to welding when things slackened off after the war before returning to the cutler's trade full time in 1952.

Ruana offers ten models of the Bowie at surprisingly modest prices, considering the amount of handwork put in each knife. Blades are made of the finest chrome alloy steel and are oil-quenched and individually heat-treated. Rudy's son-in-law, Vic Hangas, began working with him about a dozen years ago, and together they turn out knives with the pride of true craftsmen. "The feel of a knife and cutting edge, that's the main test," said Ruana. "If a knife doesn't feel right and cut right, it doesn't leave the shop. I believe in giving a man his money's worth." Ruana blades may not be quite as perfect as those of Henry, Jess Horn or others who charge three times the price, but a Ruana knife should be part of any collection. After all, Rudy has been making knives for more than half a century and is probably the oldest knifemaker still pounding steel.

Practically every knifemaker in the business offers some interpretation of the Bowie, for it would be difficult to find a knife that has captured the imagination of America's knifesmiths as it has. The Bowie, as a part of our heritage, has been a traditional challenge to the cutler and never has this challenge been better met than by today's custom makers.

Opposite, left to right: Rod Chappel modern interpretation of the Bowie with cocobolo handle; Quinton "Red" Watson Sierra Border Bowie with ebony handle and whaletooth spacer; and Chubby Hueske Bowie with polished stag grips.

chapter 8

knife collecting

Collecting knives is the kind of hobby you get into by accident rather than design, and in some ways perhaps it's closer to an obsession than a hobby.

Collectors know no boundaries of class or wealth, and somehow the knives they collect, both antique and modern, inevitably appreciate in value. As one example, old American and English Bowies have risen in value from $50 to as much as $2500 just within the past few years—such a price, of course, would be for a rare knife in good condition.

Collecting knives isn't new, and many older collectors started with such old factory knives as the old Case knives, Remington Bullets and early Winchesters. These days, however, most collectors start with modern knives.

If you want to get into collecting there are really no hard and fast rules; every man can set his own values. Modern collectors run the gamut from antique knives, foreign blades, and Samurai swords to knives of just one maker or specialized collections of skinners, general hunters or fighters.

An even more specialized kind of collecting stems from the fact that many knifemakers are a peripatetic lot, constantly on the move, with visions of a golden rainbow at the end of their quest. Many makers change their mark slightly with every move, and some collectors want an example of each period. Gil Hibben, for example, made knives in Manti, Utah; then Springdale, Arkansas; and last year moved to Anchorage, Alaska. Hibben's Manti knives are already beginning to grow in value. These were his first blades, production was fairly limited and the design of the blades was of interest. Now the Springdale production, since Hibben lived there for only a short time, is coming to be of interest to collectors.

Another factor entering the picture is that many makers are moving upward in years, and regrettably won't be making knives much longer. Both Harry Morseth and Bill Scagel passed away a few years ago. Rudy Ruana is in his mid-seventies and must be reckoned as one of the pioneers in American handcrafted knives. There are also local craftsmen, seldom known beyond a few hundred miles of their homes, who have built up remarkable trade with local sportsmen although few advertise or even care to branch out. Should a collector want to add representative work of these men he must seek them out. While this is no easy task, it does make collecting all the more absorbing for the search.

One of the most remarkable collectors, because of his enthusiasm and the size of his collection, is Phil Lobred of Anchorage, Alaska. Phil admits his great obsession is knives, although he began his collecting career with swords and bayonets. Phil doesn't seek early models of any particular maker because he refuses to collect antiques, and prefers using knives. When he cleaned out his sword collection he first began with commercial blades—Bucks, Gerbers and Pumas—since in those days it was hard to even find the names and addresses of custom cutlers. Lobred finally broke the ice by ordering a $65 Randall, which became the first knife in his new collection. As the outdoor magazines began doing articles on knifemakers, Phil started sending off for catalogs and admits he went slightly crazy for a while. "I wanted something of every maker's work and especially an interpretation of a skinning knife. If he offered a skinner I'd order that, but if he didn't have a design of his own, I'd order something with a wild curve like the old Green River knife. The wilder the curve the happier I was." Gradually Lobred evolved his own favorite type of knife, a small drop-point, full-tang Loveless style. Now he finds himself doing something he never expected when he began, turning to a flashier style of knife with ivory handles.

In general, however, Lobred sticks with working knives, and he still uses many of his knives. Lobred firmly believes the knives now being made are the finest ever seen. In spite of his emphasis on quality, Phil finds so many excellent craftsmen that it is hard to exclude any of them from his collection. When pressed, however, he admits to certain favorites, "Whenever I'm asked to show my top knives, George Herron's work is always in the group. Herron made my favorite skinner and it's a real beauty." Lloyd Hale and Bob Dozier are other makers much admired by Lobred. In Phil's opinion one of the big troubles with many of the modern knifesmiths is a lack of design orientation and the simple knowledge of just what makes a knife. Both Dozier and Hale are true designers. He also admires Bucker Gascon's work. Lobred feels he's improved his designs of late, and should become one of the important makers in coming years. Of all the knifemakers, however, Lobred regards Bob Loveless as the one man with the most appealing designs of all. Even so, he's not very partial to Loveless' Caper-Finn.

As for the care of his knives, Lobred feels that the superior steels used by name makers make it unnecessary to give much special attention to a knife. If he uses the knife he'll buff it on a machine and then just place it back in the collection. As to displaying his knives, when he first started, Phil had a display case, but as knives were added it became a bother. Now he keeps them in locked drawers. Naturally the value of any collection is higher to the owner than anyone else, but certain older models are priceless because they are impossible to replace. Lobred has a number of knives that were crafted by men no longer in the business. Since no more will ever be made, their value must eventually rise.

The opposite approach to Lobred in collecting is that of New Yorker George Miller. Miller specializes, collecting only small using knives of three to four inches, all with tapered tangs and most with ivory handles. When he began, Miller cast a long loop and tried to rope in an example from every maker he could find. After attending a couple of knife shows he received an education in knives and quickly became more selective in his taste. Realizing it just wasn't desirable to gather up one of everything in sight, since many of the knives shown were not well made, he settled on those makers whose quality met his own high standards and proceeded to trade off or sell most of his original collection.

Now specializing with a vengeance, Miller is having knives made by Bob Dozier, Morseth, Corbet Sigman and Rod Chappel that will have slab handles of both green and black jade and ruby-impregnated stone from Mexico. Asked why he collects knives, Miller, like most collectors, fumbled around for a reply and seemingly found it difficult to put into words. "I've always asked the same question of myself, and everyone who comes to my home and sees all the knives also asks the same question. They wonder why anyone wants so many of the same thing. I admit it's difficult to explain but there are few things you can buy today that show the handwork of a good maker—items that someone took time to make, and that you can be proud of owning. You can't buy an automobile you'll be proud of in that way, for under $20,000. You can order a fine gun, but a small knife is much more personal."

Miller's interest in knives began with a Loveless, and he still feels it's one of the most serviceable knives made, and one of the finest you can buy. After the 1972 knife show in Kansas City, Miller noted that most knifemakers had emulated Loveless with full-tang models, and thought it would be a good way to start his new collection. He admits now it was a mistake because many men don't do tapered tangs well, and when their knives arrived he didn't want them in his collection. Now he sticks with men whose work and standards he knows: Dozier, Morseth, Sigman, Rod Chappel and Bob Loveless. His only using knife is a Morseth; the forty-odd others are for his perusal and pleasure.

As to the hazards of ivory cracking and splitting, Miller uses baby oil and nose oil that comes from just rubbing the handle against the side of his nose, as he does with a pipe to bring out the grain. The oil seems to feed the pores of ivory and gives excellent protection against cracking. To protect the blades he takes a jeweler's cloth and chamois and wipes them down about twice a week. On occasion a small amount of oil of cloves will be rubbed on the steel for protection.

Since the collecting of contemporary knives is relatively new, information is still hard to obtain. Andy Russell puts out a *Knife Collector's Newsletter* that comes out six times a year, and a bi-monthly knife magazine, *The American Blade,* has just been born, but for the most part, knife collectors have to go their own way, learning, searching and asking questions.

Knives from the George Miller collection. These are small "using" knives with ivory handles from the shops of many outstanding craftsmen. Miller feels that he made a mistake in insisting on ivory, because it shrinks and cracks. Future knives added to his collection will be of ivory Micarta.

More fine blades from the George Miller collection, including a miniature Bowie and a large hunter with handle of black Cape buffalo horn.

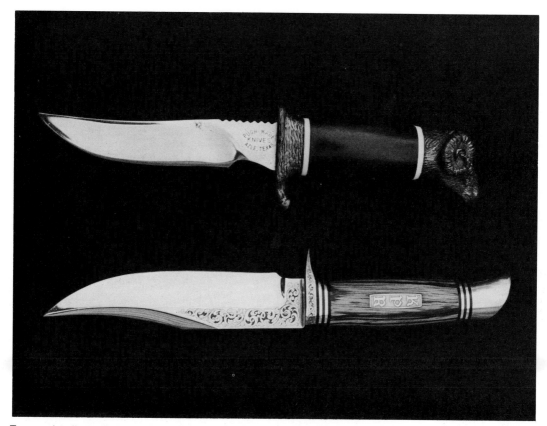

Two real collector's items. Top knife by Jim Pugh, bottom by Harvey Draper.

Of course it isn't really all that difficult. Let's consider the average hunter for a moment. If he owns one knife, and he likes knives, he'll soon decide that a small skinner or caper might make a fine addition and certainly ease his life on a hunt. If he's gone this far a boning knife might be next. Then when springtime comes, guns go back in the cabinet, and a fishing rod is picked up, like a bolt from the blue the thought occurs that none of these knives is a fillet knife. Suddenly, without even realizing it, our friend becomes a collector. In the beginning he's got an excuse, because each of these highly specialized blades does serve a utilitarian purpose and may be obtained without too many pangs of conscience. What sportsman ever needed an excuse for another knife or another gun?

A true collector, on the other hand, will admit his passion and get on with the job of collecting, ignoring all obstacles in his path. Depending on the personality of the budding collector, as much pleasure and fun may be had from collecting haphazardly as being highly organized. Certain standards of quality should be set before running off in a dozen different directions, but the basic question is, what do you want to collect?

One of the most personal things you can carry with you is a knife, and one of the most pleasurable things you can have in your den is a fine collection of knives. If you like knives there is no time like the present for collecting. The main thing is to begin—and enjoy.

chapter 9

knife care

When I first became involved with knifemakers and started discussing the various methods of placing an edge on a blade, I thought back to my grandfather and the fascination I had as a small boy with his preparations for shaving. First his straight razor would be honed on a whetstone lubricated with oil, for my grandfather was a machinist and toolmaker and knew about such things. Then, exercising great care and precision, he would slowly draw the blade back and forth, occasionally testing it with his thumb until the sharpness suited his pleasure. The razor would then be stropped a couple of times on a leather strap hanging near the washbasin, and as a final gesture he'd gently strop it again across the palm of his hand a few times. After a generous lathering he was ready for the big show, by which time I usually sat in silent terror at the thought of that wicked-looking edge being drawn across bare skin. I can attest to the daring and skill of my granddad, for he never cut himself in all the years I watched this act of bravery and I still recall it with admiration and respect.

As I slowly learned the skills of honing a blade I discovered that my grandfather's method is still the best. If done correctly it would obviate the common fear of knifemakers that their blades will be ruined, not by use, but by improper sharpening.

Most people, when they think about sharpening a knife, think of emulating their neighborhood butcher, using a long hone steel. However, butcher knives are usually made of soft steel and the few swipes taken merely touch up the edges. Hunting knives, on the contrary, have very hard and durable edges and it's a different process altogether. There are some excellent hone steels

for sportsmen made by Gerber and Schrade Walden which come in neat leather cases that form a handle for use. However, with hunting knives these hones are used mainly as a file to establish a bevel or touch up an edge in the field. They will sharpen a knife well but they should not be used as the primary instrument for placing a final edge on your knife.

The majority of knives delivered from a master cutler arrive already sharpened, but in spite of the tales of some mythical blade that skinned six moose, four deer and countless elephant without being resharpened, any knife, all claims to the contrary, will require sharpening during its lifetime. Accordingly, when you lay out your hard-earned money for a fine knife you may as well go the whole route and acquire first-rate sharpening gear at the same time.

The finest stone is none too good to complement your handmade knife and keep it in working trim, and a good whetstone is still the preferred method of placing an edge on your knife and keeping it there. Whether you are sharpening a $200 custom knife or a store-bought pocket folder, a top-quality bench stone is the one prime requisite for doing the job correctly. Knifemakers seem to argue about almost everything in knifedom, but there is general agreement on A. G. Russell's Washita/Soft Arkansas Oilstones, and many knifesmiths carry them in their catalogs. The Russell stone is a carefully graded novaculite, a natural whetstone found in a small area of Arkansas and used by the majority of knifemakers. One of the reasons these stones have become so popular is that Russell is known to discard over 80 percent of the material quarried and cut, and sells only the finest quality.

The care of your knife is basically simple, requiring less labor than cleaning a firearm, for example, yet you will need a few bits and pieces of proper equipment to do the work right and a fair amount of practice before you'll be able to put a professional edge to your knife.

When buying your first stone a good rule of thumb to follow is to obtain one an inch or two longer than the blades of the knives you intend to sharpen. These stones will probably last a lifetime, so the investment of a few extra dollars is worthwhile. Since you will be using both hands to guide the knife and place pressure on it when sharpening, a stone mount is an important accessory. The mount holds the stone firmly, and you can use a C-clamp to fasten the rig securely on a work bench or table. The third and final item is a good-quality honing oil. Whetstones should never be used dry and you should never use an oil containing molybdenum disulfide or graphite, for these will eventually clog the surface and glaze the stone. Either Norton's Bear Oil or Russell's Sharpening & Honing Oil is recommended. The job of the oil is to float the tiny particles of steel shavings above the surface of the stone and allow the blade edge to move smoothly.

When you're ready to sharpen, begin with a clean knife. If you've just returned from a hunting trip, wash the blade with soap and water and then dry it thoroughly, otherwise you will grind fat, blood and dirt into the stone's surface and ruin it. With the blade clean begin by pouring a liberal amount of oil onto the stone, making certain the entire area is covered. (Smear it about with your fingers until the surface is covered. Oil is cheap, and it's better to

Overleaf: A. G. Russell checks the edge of a knife, a full-tang model by Bob Dozier.

use too much rather than too little.) Then, holding the handle of your knife with both hands, place the blade to your right with the heel resting on the stone at a 20-degree angle. Bearing down hard, draw the blade across the stone in a slicing motion from heel to point so you end up with the tip of the knife on the stone. As you near the curve toward the point, slightly change or lift the angle in order to maintain an even edge to the very tip. And remember to bear down hard. As Andy Russell says, "gentle swipes will do nothing but make you feel good. It's important to use as much pressure as possible, this cannot be overemphasized, and not to rock the blade as you draw it across the stone."

After your first stroke, reverse the knife and repeat the same action from left to right. Do this, alternating sides, for ten or fifteen times, then check the edge. It may be that the curve toward the tip will not be quite as sharp as the straight part of the blade. If this is the case, then repeat the action, paying particular attention to those portions of the blade that don't suit you.

Russell points out that "the angle you use is not quite as important as being able to hold and maintain the *same angle* stroke after stroke. Only practice gives this ability, and you should practice on your wife's kitchen knives first. Not only will you save your good knives until you learn these skills, but she'll be pleased to have sharp kitchen cutlery for a change."

This angle, incidentally, like so many things in knifemaking, is a small matter of dispute, but you'll find the majority of knifemakers grinding their bevel roughly to a 20-degree angle. If you're really fussy, take a small protractor and check it out before you start. When you have finished the blade to your satisfaction strop it across the palm of your hand or on a piece of cardboard. This last final touch lays any roughness down in line with the edge.

Perhaps the most important point in sharpening a knife is knowing when to stop. Remember, you don't make a knife any sharper by honing to a finer bevel; you only weaken the blade. When sharpening a hunting knife you aren't seeking an edge like a surgeon's scalpel, and the man who expects a comfortable shave from his knife must realize that same edge won't be practical in the field dressing game. All things being equal, the finer the edge the faster the blade will dull, and you soon reach the point of diminishing returns. Knifemakers and experienced hunters agree that a slightly coarse edge is to be preferred. By this we don't mean an edge that appears rough to the eye or touch (although a microscope will reveal small sawteeth on the sharpest blade) but rather an edge that is the result of proper honing and stropping. Should you be among the many who insist upon shaving with your benchmade knife, a stunt that proves nothing actually, a few strokes across an Arkansas Surgical Black Stone will do the trick nicely and let you shave your arm.

When you have completed your sharpening, the stone should be cleaned. This is done by pouring additional oil onto the surface and smearing it about with your fingers to let the steel filings removed by sharpening become loose and float on the surface. A few wipes with a rag and you're ready the next time your knife needs attention. Should the stone become very dirty just take an old toothbrush and kerosene, or a good household cleanser, and give it a good scrubbing, then set it aside to dry.

Remember the few rules of placing an edge on your knife: (1) maintain the bevel ground onto the blade by the knifemaker; (2) *slice* across the stone as though you were cutting a piece of cheese, taking an equal number of strokes in both directions; (3) when a knife becomes dull, even slightly dull, sharpen it *now!*

Accessories to aid in keeping an edge on your knife. Honing steels are by Gerber and Schrade-Walden. The long thin rod is a Moon Stick by Case, an excellent tool for quick touchup. The large white sharpening stone is a Washita/Soft Arkansas stone, and the large black one is the Surgical Black to be used as a final touch for razorlike sharpness. The loupe is for examining the blade edge. Russell's oil may be purchased quite inexpensively in large cans.

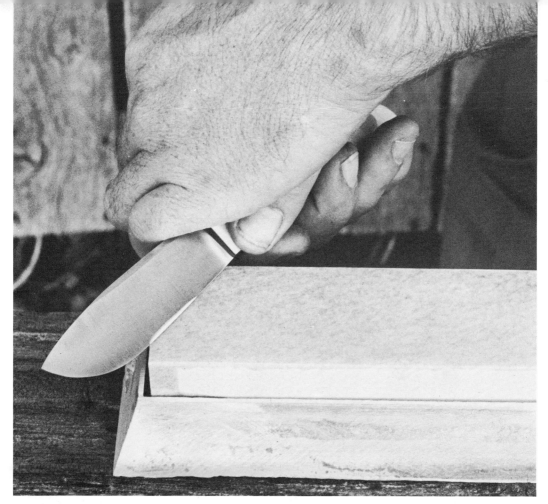

A well-oiled Washita/Soft stone set in a stone cradle. Grasp the knife in both hands to maintain the angle of attack, bearing down **hard.**

Continue across the stone, maintaining pressure all the time as though you were slicing cheese, and draw the knife slowly toward you.

As you near the end of the stone raise the edge slightly in order to sharpen the point toward the tip.

Reverse the knife and draw it across in the opposite direction. Always begin with the heel of the knife in the lower corner of the stone.

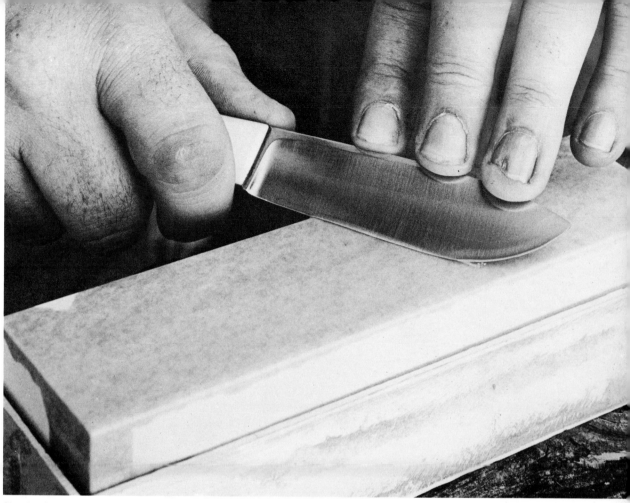

Slowly draw the knife across the stone, remembering to bear down hard. Note fine roll of oil in front of the blade.

Again, as you near the edge, raise the knife a bit to sharpen the point.

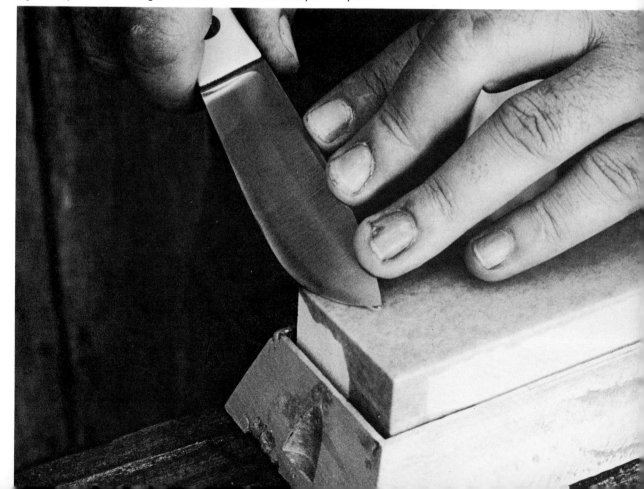

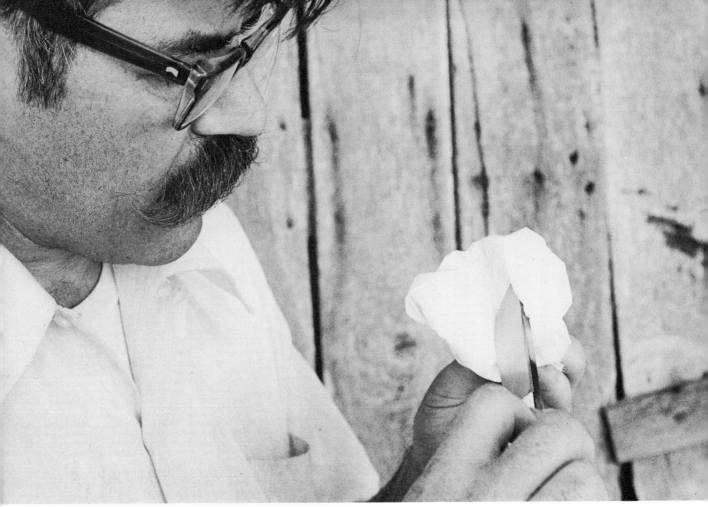

A. G. Russell, who demonstrated this series, now wipes oil from the blade.

A final strop across the palm of your hand or on a piece of cardboard will set the edge.

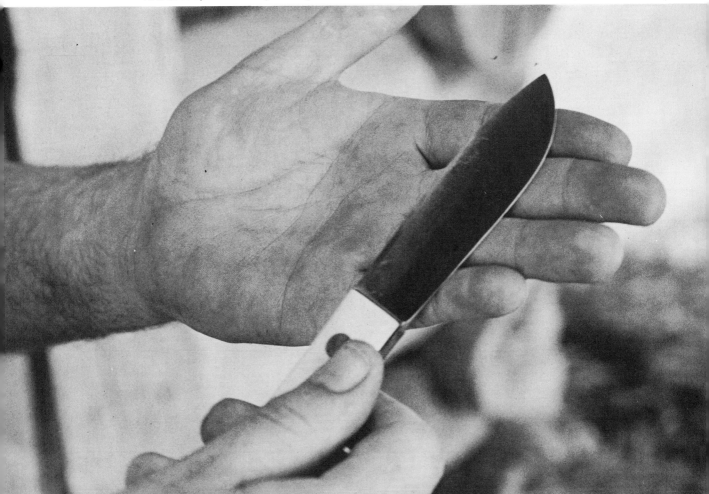

Russell draws the sharpened blade across his thumbnail. If the knife slides smoothly the job is done.

When sharpening is completed a dash of fresh oil and a wipe with a rag will clean the stone and leave it in good condition for next time.

What of the pocket stones you often see riding kangaroo-style in a pouch attached to the sheath? These are fine for a quick touchup in the field, but are not suited for a proper honing. There may be times when you find yourself far from camp, dressing game with the winter sun setting swiftly over the distant hills. You are tired from hours of hunting, and as you slice and skin the knife seems to be dragging and taking more effort. That is the time to pull out the small pocket stone and touch up the edge. What about oil? Hell, spit on it, rub snow over the surface or smear a bit of the carcass on at times like this. Don't be fussy, but keep the blade sharp.

When it comes to the care of a handmade knife, it's more a matter of don'ts than dos. Never throw your knife, although the temptation may be great. Don't chop with your knife, unless it's specifically designed for the purpose like the back of George Stone's Magnum Hunter. (Or carry one of the small hand axes offered by a number of makers or an inexpensive folding saw.) Don't use your fine knife as a general-purpose tool for prying open cans or tightening screws on your guns. It's poor economy to use a fine knife as a cheap tool. The cardinal rule is that a good blade, carefully honed, is for cutting hide and tissue and should never be used for any other purpose. Ultimately, you are the sole judge of just how much punishment you will give your knife, or how much you expect it to take. With reasonable care a fine knife should last a lifetime.

Another question is, what do you do with your knife after hunting season? Well, one thing you don't do is shove it in a sheath and put it in a closet or bottom drawer. Actually, storing of knives has always been a problem not only to sportsmen but to collectors and museums. There are few rules to follow and even these aren't infallible; I've seen some of my favorite blades pit and rust after receiving the greatest care and attention. Knife sheaths, like gun scabbards, are usually made of leather which collects moisture and gives off fumes of tanning acids. This is the last place to store your knife. High humidity and salt air are added hazards to a knife, and the climate you live in will have much to do with the well-being of your knife. The best method, if you have a fancy display piece, is to keep it lightly oiled and hang it on the wall. One collector I know has a small glass-enclosed coffee table and keeps his knives safely displayed where he can enjoy them. A few bits of silica gel in a fancy container set inside the case dries up moisture.

Andy Russell's advice on storing knives is to clean them well, rub a light coating of oil on the blades, then wrap them in waxed paper. A more exotic method of knife care used by collectors of Japanese weaponry is offered by the Japanese Sword Company of Tokyo. This simple yet fascinating kit contains a small buffer resembling a powder puff or lollypop on a stick. It contains a fine pumice powder and is tapped on the blade to remove rust spots. Small squares of rice paper are used for wiping down the blade, and a bottle containing Japanese oil of cloves is used for coating the blade for protection. Incidentally, when you start using oil of cloves you are getting into the big leagues of knife collecting. There is a photograph of the kit on page 151.

Knife handles present few problems except for ivory and buffalo horn. Ivory is one of the most beautiful and traditional materials, but it's also one of the most frustrating and infuriating. It will split, crack and eventually show tiny hairlines. With age it will darken down naturally with golden-yellow tones and

An excellent aid for those who may have trouble maintaining the correct angle when sharpening is the Buck Honemaster. It won't harm your blade, since the inside of the clamp is covered with rubber. The blade is inserted and tightened with a thumbscrew. The knife here is by Rod Chappel.

become quite handsome if you can keep it in one piece long enough to reach this stage. Bob Dozier suggests that a new ivory-handled knife should be rubbed every other day with baby oil for about six months, at which point you stop and pray. The theory is that new ivory, and buffalo horn, too, is porous and constantly shrinking and moving against retaining pins and epoxy. The oil helps to fill the pores so the ivory can flex without too much harm. When I first heard of this I deliberately made a test by treating one ivory-handled knife as per direction while leaving another similar knife untouched. In this case, the untreated handle has developed splits while its companion is still in satisfactory condition at the end of six months.

All things considered, just use ordinary common sense, and remember that a handcrafted knife should be treated with a modicum of respect and receive a modest amount of attention. If you want to cut steel, get a bandsaw, or as one knifemaker said, "If you want to punch holes in silver dollars get a drill press—it does a better job." Use your knife for its intended purpose. Take care of it, and you'll receive many years of service.

chapter 10

sheaths and custom decoration

Two aspects of knifemaking that do not necessarily fall within the maker's province but that certainly deserve a place in this book are sheath making and fancy blade decoration, such as engraving, damascening and etching.

Most makers provide sheaths with their knives for its basic price, and most of them craft these sheaths themselves. It's only fair to say, however, that of all the tasks involved, sheath-making is probably the most hateful task for knifemakers. Not only is it time-consuming, but with rare exceptions, knife-smiths don't like leatherworking.

"In fact," Bob Loveless admits, "I'm so damn happy to make a fine knife and find it come out right I'm worn out when it comes to sheaths. If the public would get over their hangups on the use of traditional materials we could all improve tremendously in the field of plastics. Fiber is the very best liner material, as used in the Morseth or Kneubuhler sheaths, and it will have to do until we're allowed to move into other materials." Corbet Sigman concurs, saying, "I honestly resent the time I devote to making a sheath since it could be put to better use making another knife blade, but I suppose I'll have to go along with this, since we must supply some means of carrying a knife safely."

The sad thing is that very often this subconscious attitude is reflected in the work, though certainly not in Loveless' or Sigman's case. Many sheaths are too large and bulky, and well below the quality of the knives they accom-

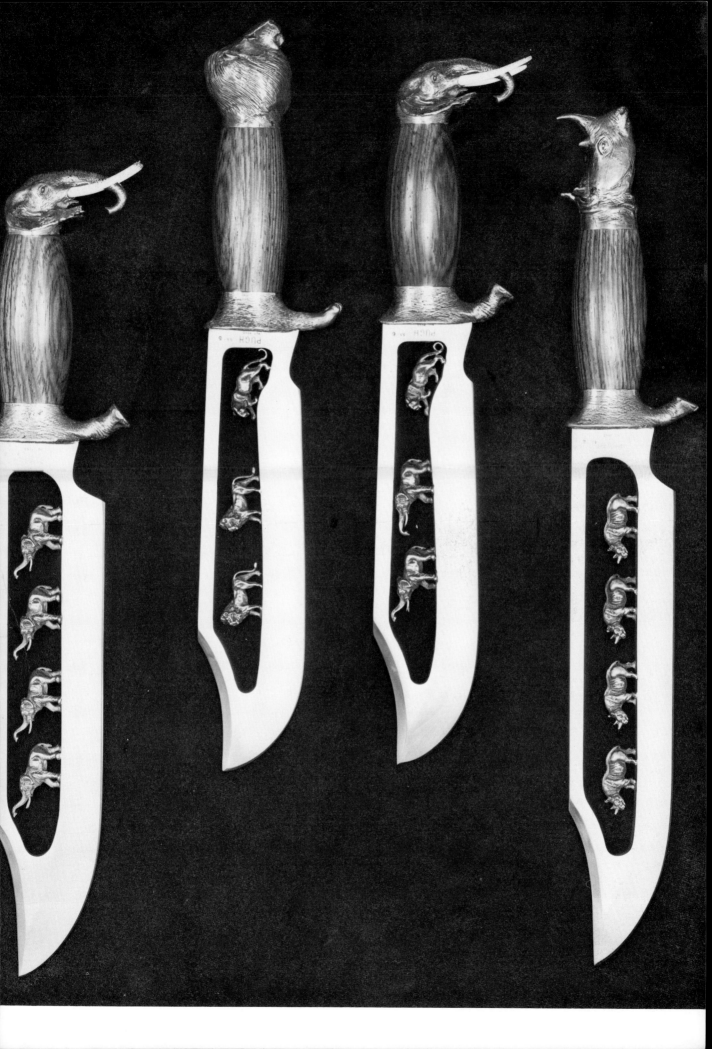

pany. In general, knifemakers should take a look at the kind of work done by the better gun holster makers, men like Paris Theodore of Seventrees, Ltd. in New York. Theodore normally makes only gun holsters and specializes in what he calls no-nonsense rigs for the professional who lays his life on the line. He does make one knife holster, for the Loveless Boot knife, and it is an unusual shoulder rig. However, many of Theodore's concepts, particularly in the quick-draw line, could readily be adapted to knives. For example, a slight forward cant, say 45 degrees, would be a great convenience in a knife sheath, yet to my knowledge, nobody makes one. A knife should be simply drawn from any sheath and be retained just as simply. The Morseth sheath, with its fiber liner, is a tremendous improvement over many current models. You may safely store your knife in this sheath and the blade is completely surrounded by rust-preventing fiber, which protects both the knife and the wearer. The WK sheath also protects the wearer and is an excellent sheath.

Another particularly good sheath is George Stone's model; if it had a liner it would be ideal from almost every point of view. It's small, light, rides high enough on your hip and your knife is convenient to draw. I'm afraid, however, that the majority of knifemakers will continue making sheaths as an afterthought. And I'm not really sure I blame them.

Special engraved, etched or even sculptured blade decoration lies outside the capability of most knifemakers, and is generally added later by another hand, just as in the case of gun engraving. As a matter of fact, knife engraving is often considered an offshoot of gun engraving, and many gun engravers undertake knife work as well.

Actually, however, engraving a knife blade isn't quite as simple and easy as working on guns. For one thing, knife steel is much harder and the engraver must exercise really exceptional care. Henry Frank, a gun engraver before he became a knifesmith, and one of the few who does his own work, says that knife steels raise absolute hell with tools, requiring resharpening to avoid the errors that come from dull tools. In addition, a knife blade isn't as solid as the receiver on a gun and vibrates with each hammer tap. To eliminate this problem Frank designed a series of special chisel blocks to hold the blade firmly. Even so, he finds that he must pace himself and can't work as rapidly as he would engraving a gun.

Frank is famous for his magnificent detail and executes both scroll and high relief engraving on both blade and metal parts of the handle. The fine work of game heads (which run the gamut from mountain lion to deer) is done entirely with hand tools, gently removing minute pieces of metal until the design is completed. Unfortunately Frank's splendid work is obtained only on special order and is usually done on his knives alone.

Frank's work is impressive and his skills in the art of knifemaking, combined with the difficult art of engraving, are equally developed. His knives are works of art in the traditional sense, but are also intended for serious use, and he has sold his work out of the Loveless shop since 1971.

Another gunsmith and one of the finest young engravers to come to our shores is Lynton McKenzie, who arrived from Australia via Purdey, Holland

Overleaf: Jim Pugh's handsome set of knives with African game animals in gold. Hilts and butts are also of gold, and the heads are inlaid with precious stones in the eyes and ivory tusks.

& Holland and other fine London gunmakers. McKenzie's hobby was antique guns and arms restoration, and he got into the gun trade when a Sydney gunsmith botched some work for him. Now working for the New Orleans Arms Company, McKenzie is still primarily a gun engraver, but he has done some magnificent work on fine knives. Andy Russell owns some of McKenzie's work and compares him with the finest engravers ever to come down the pike. Prices for Lynton's work, like that of most engravers, depend on the individual design and the amount of work.

Another very skilled engraver (and, at thirty-three, a very young one also) is Winston C. Churchill, a native of Vermont who engraves firearms for Griffin & Howe, the New York gunsmithing firm. Winston is in the very first rank of

Another selection of Pugh's work. The top knife has a handle of ivory and ebony with gold rhino head; the center is also ebony; and the bottom knife is cocobolo.

engravers in the United States, and he does magnificent work. I recently saw a heavy Bone folding knife he had worked on; the brass frame was profusely engraved, and the ivory scales were hand-checkered like a fine gunstock.

A somewhat simpler and more economical method of knife decoration is practiced by Sherill Shaw and Leonard Leibowitz, a young husband-and-wife team. They use the ancient method of acid etching, a technique that goes back to medieval times and is done today exactly as it always was. The steel is covered with a mixture of Egyptian asphalt and beeswax and the pattern is then scribed into the wax freehand, leaving those areas exposed to the action of the acid. One advantage of this style of etching is that the type or condition of the steel offers no obstacle. It may be worked in any condition, tempered or untempered, high-carbon or stainless, because the action of the acid is universal and not significantly influenced by the type of steel involved.

Thus modern steels with high Rockwell ratings, which are difficult or impossible for most engravers to work with, offer no problem for Shaw-Leibowitz. In fact, they may even obtain sharper definition on these steels.

The technique of acid etching goes back to the beginning of arms decoration itself. The early Nuremberg engravers, Hans Holbein and Albrecht Dürer, both worked for Emperor Maximilian I of Germany, who had in his employ the finest artisans and armorers of his day. This is the tradition that Shaw-Leibowitz are trying to revive, applying modern technology to the traditional techniques of an old profession. They admit to encountering some prejudice regarding acid etching because of uneven work done in the past. Now, for example, they can stop the etching process on any outline on the steel in order to make it lighter or darker and to emphasize certain lines. Different tones may also be placed on the metal, and this allows control unheard-of until recently. They now work to three different visual tones and obtain three different depths in the metal as well. This delicate modeling and quality has rarely been achieved in the past. Practically any type of picture can be done and detail is so fine they may even portray a recognizable likeness of the subject or a figure from history.

The fanciest form of knife decoration of all is that featured by Texan Jim Pugh. Strictly for collectors, rather than using knives, it might be called "silhouette sculpture" and the amount of work it requires makes blades so decorated the costliest of all. Jim began making knives during World War II from old files, but didn't get into professional knifemaking until many years later. His latest creative effort is a set of four blades with cut-outs showing marching lines of African game animals in gold. Guard and pommel are also gold and the carved heads are set with semi-precious stones. Are you ready for the price? $24,000 per set.

Of course, if you'll settle for something less expensive, his Model 3 knife is a fairly simple affair with engraved blade, gold sheep's head butt and a half-carat diamond set in each eye. The price for this beauty is only $5000. Fortunately, not all of Pugh's prizes are quite so expensive; his basic charge is $200 for anything in bronze, running up the scale through sterling silver to green, pink and yellow gold. His blades are 440-C stainless and a list of handle materials includes exotic woods, buffalo horn and ivory. One interesting thing about Pugh's knives is that guards and pommels are solid and not plated. This

Cross section of the Morseth sheath, showing the fiber liner encasing the knife. This method of construction protects the knife from rust as well as the wearer from danger in falls.

can be done because Jim works with the most modern jewelry equipment available.

Jim got into knifemaking when he decided there should be something different on the market, and after a thorough survey, he decided on these artistic designs, combined with precious stones and crafted of rare metals. I'd say they're something different, and then some!

Primarily a gun engraver, Alvin A. White of Sandwich, Massachusetts, is no newcomer to the art of engraving blades. Some of the most handsome Bowies have been done by White (from blades by Ron Wilson) with ivory scales and gold guards. Now in his early fifties, White has been a gun engraver for over twenty years. He got his first professional training in his home city of Attleboro during the Depression when a jewelry trade school was opened and has gone on from there to engraving firearms, tomahawks and knives. Besides collecting firearms and armor of colonial times, White occasionally restores antique guns and edged weapons. He is a true master engraver.

Now, what of the future of handmade blades? Steels will undoubtedly improve, and while a knife may last a lifetime and be handed down from father

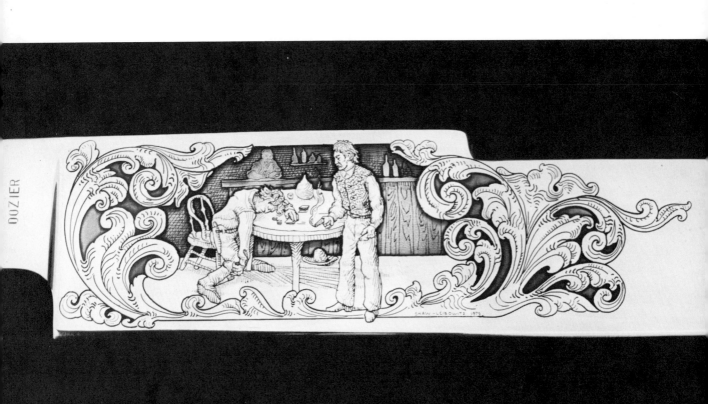

The exquisite work of Shaw-Leibowitz, showing the fine detail and shading on two of Bob Dozier's Bowies.

to son, the latter may not be satisfied with dad's gift a dozen years hence. Visitors to knife shows these past few years have seen phenomenal strides in skill and design. Knifemakers like Chubby Hueske, George Herron, Jess Horn and Frank Centofante were doing professional work when they arrived on the scene, as were Ron Lake and Don Zaccagnino. The fine makers will undoubtedly prosper as they become ever more artful in crafting knives. Others, sadly, will never improve but will continue to make the same shoddy knives and eventually drift into another business. The same can be said of those who treat their customers with disdain.

What kind of a knife should you buy? Sorry, but I can't tell you that now any more than I could earlier. I don't know your likes and dislikes, or, for that matter, your skills with a knife. I will say this, however: anything beyond four and a half inches is, in my opinion, too much knife for a using hunting knife. I also prefer a hilt to prevent cut fingers, though the wild and wooly hilt gimmicks are just too impractical for sporting use. But you're the buyer, so get whatever appeals to you. Keep in mind too that not every famous maker is still producing the excellent blades his reputation was built upon, and much fine craftsmanship is coming from shops of younger men who still haven't received their fair share of renown.

Such great names as Cooper, Loveless, Moran, Randall and Morseth are still up there with the best, turning out fine knives and striving to maintain well-deserved reputations built over long years. But many newer makers deserve your attention too, because the knives they craft are among the finest in the world.

Perhaps you are not yet convinced that there is much point in owning a

R. W. Wilson Bowie engraved by Alvin A. White, one of America's foremost gun engravers. The handle is of ivory and gold with fine scrollwork on hilt and butt cap.

A Texas Ranger commemorative tomahawk, made by R. W. Wilson, well known for his replicas of trade tomahawks, and engraved by Alvin A. White.

Knives by Gerry Jean of Manchester, Conn.

A selection of sheaths, typical of the many styles offered by various makers. From left to right: Dan Dennehy pouch sheath; Morseth sheath covered with zebra; George Stone sheath; Bob Loveless pouch sheath with adjustable loop; another Morseth sheath covered with leopard; and Don Zaccagnino model that partially protects the handle with quick-release thong.

handmade knife. Well, I have always felt the man who makes a fine shot with a rifle and brings down a trophy deserves something more than a $10 knife to complement his gun. That is my personal justification for the benchmade knife.

appendix:

knifemakers and suppliers

Beginning in late 1969, knifemaking in the United States moved into a new era marked by the appearance of many new craftsmen offering a great variety of knives to the public.

As that year drew to a close, Bob Loveless, the well-known California maker, and Andy Russell, the Arkansas purveyor of sharpening stones, met in Loveless' shop and discussed this tremendous surge of knifemaking and laid plans for a showing of knives which subsequently took place in Las Vegas in February 1970. Further discussion among knifemakers present at that gathering seemed to indicate a strong sentiment for additional shows, and A. G. Russell then arranged for another show to be held in Tulsa, Oklahoma, in May 1970. It was at the Tulsa show that the eleven knifemakers present formed the Knifemakers Guild, at a meeting chaired by Bob Loveless, who was elected founding secretary. Andy Russell was elected honorary president of the newly formed Guild.

The 1971 show was held in Houston in August, and another score of knifemakers joined the original eleven members in putting on a very successful exhibit. The purposes of the Guild were then and remain today to enhance handmade knives and their makers; to assist the knifemakers technically; to affirm the ethical values of knifemaking; and to put on, once each year in varying locations of the country, an annual knife show and business meeting.

1972 saw the show being held at the Muehlebach Hotel in Kansas City in conjunction with the Missouri Valley Arms Collectors Association, and it was held there again in mid-August 1973.

Of particular interest to the knife-buying public was the formation of a technical committee at the last Guild meeting. Corbet Sigman, Dan Dennehy, Lloyd Hale and Bob Loveless were elected members of this standing committee to pass on the quality of work offered by prospective members and to advise and guide those who may need a helping hand in some particularly elusive skill.

Voting membership in the Knifemakers Guild is open to any knifemaker who offers his work to the general public and who has printed a catalog of his work. New members are accepted for a probationary period of one year at the annual business meeting, and full membership comes the following year by an acceptance vote of a majority of those members present.

While the business of knifemaking has inevitably seen certain abuses of the customer's trust on the part of a few knifemakers, it should be pointed out the Guild can make no warranty for or about any individual knifemaker concerning the quality of his work or his business methods.

Knives available from Guild members range in price from under $20 to well over $500, and the discerning buyer should be able to obtain honest value for his money. The Guild also invites comment from anyone who fails to obtain satisfaction in dealing with knifemakers, or who encounters problems with any member knifemaker. Bill Moran, the present secretary, will relinquish his post to a new member who will be elected at the 1973 meeting and who will hold office for the ensuing year.

Knifemakers, by their very nature, are a group of rugged individualists, but many of them have joined the Guild, and there is little doubt that the formation of the Guild has done much to upgrade quality, craftsmanship and ethics in a very short time. The asterisks in the following list of knifemakers indicate Guild membership as of May 1973.

Note: With rare exceptions, most knifemakers run small, one-man shops and make every effort to trim costs where it doesn't count. Catalogs cost money, and it's suggested that you enclose 50 cents for each one you request. Rod Chappel, Dan Dennehy, Ted Dowell and Bob Loveless all charge $1, and D. E. Henry requests $3 for a set of photographs of his knives.

In most instances these costs are refundable if you order a knife. Many catalogs are simply single sheets listing or showing the knives and prices, while others are small booklets containing the knifemaker's thoughts on steels, method of crafting a knife and philosophy of knifemaking. These are excellent and will give you a general education regarding knives and steels.

Bill Bagwell
Box 869
Vivian, La. 71082

Baker Knives
Box 514 B
Hinsdale, Ill. 60521

Barbee Knives
Box 1702
Ft. Stockton, Tex. 79735

* Ralph Bone
806 Avenue J
Lubbock, Tex. 79401

* Lou Booth
16 Cypress Terrace
Boonton, N.J. 07005

H. G. Bourne
1252 Hope Ave.
Columbus, Ohio 43212

* Bowen Knife Co.
593 Westminster Dr. N.E.
Atlanta, Ga. 30324

Lynn Brown
301 East Neece St.
Long Beach, Calif. 90805

* Ray Busch
940 Orion Ave.
Metaire, La. 70005

Peter Callan, Jr.
7813 River Rd.
Wagerman, La. 70094

* Frank Centofante
Box 17587
Tampa, Fla. 33612

* Rod Chappel
Davis Custom Knives
North 1405 Ash
Spokane, Wash. 99201

* John Nelson Cooper
Box 1423
Burbank, Calif. 91505

Harold Corby
Rt. 3, Lynn Rd.
Johnson City, Tenn. 37601

Dave Cosby
1016 Cliff Dr. Apt. 111
Santa Barbara, Calif.

* Don Couchman
Star Route
La Mesa, N.M. 88044

Crawford Knives
205 N. Center
West Memphis, Ark. 72301

Steve Davenport
301 Meyer
Alvin, Tex. 77511

Larry Davis
411 Cedar Drive
Pierce, Idaho 83546

W. C. Davis
Box 96, Rt. 2
Raymore, Mo. 64083

Phillip Day
Rt. 1, Box 465T
Bay Minette, Ala. 36507

Gary Decker
2207 Greenwell
Baton Rouge, La. 70805

* Dan Dennehy
Box 4479
Yuma, Ariz. 85364

Norman Dew
742 Nobhollow
Channelview, Tex. 77530

Charles Dickey
803 Northeast A St.
Bentonville, Ark. 72712

* T. M. Dowell
139 St. Helens Pl.
Bend, Ore. 97701

* Bob Dozier
P.O. Box 58
Palmetto, La. 71358

* Gene Dumatrait
Rt. 1, Box 42
Orange, Tex. 77630

John Ek
1547 N.W. 119th St.
North Miami, Fla. 33142

Faulconer Knives
Rt. 3
Frederick, Okla. 73542

* Clyde Fischer
Rt. 1, Box 170–M
Victoria, Tex. 77901

C. S. Fitch
1755 Laurel St.
Baton Rouge, La. 70802

* H. H. Frank
1 Mountain Meadow Rd.
Whitefish, Mont. 59937

A. J. Freiling
4082 Adams Ct.
Wheaton, Md. 20902

James Furlow
4838 Santa Fe Trail
Atlanta, Ga. 30340

* Bucker Gascon
1848 Bench Boulevard
Billings, Mont. 59101

Clay Gault
1626 Palma Plaza
Austin, Tex. 78703

Robert Gess
Wolfe Point
Mont. 59201

* Wayne Goddard
473 Durham Ave.
Eugene, Ore. 79402

Jim Grow
1712 Carlisle Rd.
Oklahoma City, Okla. 73120

* Lloyd Hale
609 Henrietta St.
Springdale, Ark. 72764

Oscar Harwood
903 S. Cooper St.
Memphis, Tenn. 38104

* Don Hastings
Detroit, Tex. 75436

Tommy Having
1549 27th St. N.
Huey Town, Ala. 54986

* Pete Heath
119 Grant St.
Winneconne, Wis. 54986

* D. E. Henry
Star Route
Mountain Ranch, Calif. 95246

* George Herron
920 Murrah Ave.
Aiken, S.C. 29801

* Gil Hibben
Box 3914
Anchorage, Alaska 99501

Dean Holder
6808 N. 30th Dr.
Phoenix, Ariz. 85017

* Jess Horn
Box 1274
Redding, Calif. 96001

* Chubby Hueske
4808 Tamarisk Dr.
Bellaire, Tex. 77401

* Jerry Hunt
4606 Princeton
Garland, Tex. 75040

Billy Mace Imel
945 Jamison Ct.
New Castle, Ind. 47362

Gerry Jean
6330 Center St.
Manchester, Conn. 06040

Ruffin Johnson
742 Edgebrook Dr.
Houston, Tex. 77034

J. Fred Jones
858 East I St.
Ontario, Calif. 91762

Gary Kelley
4100 S.W. 99th
Beaverton, Ore. 97005

Robert L. Kellogg
Rt. 4, Box 181
Monroe, La. 71201

* Jon Kirk
800 N. Olive St.
Fayetteville, Ark. 72701

* Walter Kneubuhler
P. O. Box 327
Pioneer, Ohio 43554

* Ron Lake
38 Illini Dr.
Taylorville, Ill. 62568

Steve Landers
3817 N.W. 125th St.
Oklahoma City, Okla.

Lane Bros.
Rt. 5
Carbondale, Ill. 62901

John LeBlanc
P.O. Box 81
Sulphur, La. 70663

L. B. Lienenmann
635 Grand Ave.
Billings, Mont. 59102

* Jimmy Lile
Rt. 1
Russelville, Ark. 72801

LOF Knives
Rt. 1, Box 286
Lakeside, Ariz. 85929

Ronald H. Little
160 Marion Drive
Ringgold, Ga. 30736

* R. W. Loveless
Box 7836, Arlington Sta.
Riverside, Calif. 92503

Robert Ludwig
1028 Pecos Ave.
Port Arthur, Tex. 77640

Jerry McAlphin
Bullard, Tex. 75757

H. McBurnette
Rt. 4, Box 337
Piedmont, Ala. 36272

Harry K. McEvoy
2155 Tremont Blvd. N.W.
Grand Rapids, Mich. 49504

Joe Martin
Box 6552
Lubbock, Tex. 79413

Max Meyer
418 Jolee
Richardson, Tex. 75080

* John Mims
620 S. 28th Ave.
Hattiesburg, Miss. 39401

Mitchell Knives
511 Ave. B South
Houston, Tex. 77587

Randall Made Knives
Box 1988
Orlando, Fla. 32802

Jim Smith
8924 Roller
Wichita, Kan. 67212

* William Moran, Jr.
Rt. 5
Frederick, Md. 21701

R. J. Read, Jr.
519 Catalina Dr.
Nashville, Tenn. 37217

* John T. Smith
6048 Cedar Crest Dr.
Southaven, Miss. 38671

* Morseth Knives
1705 Highway 71 N.
Springdale, Ark. 72764

* Charles Richardson
Box 38329
Dallas, Tex. 75238

W. J. Sonneville
1050 Chalet Dr. West
Mobile, Ala. 36608

* Jim Mustin
Cajun Knives
Box 149
Liverty, Miss. 39645

Joe Rodriquez
5241 Josephine St.
Lynwood, Calif. 90262

* Bernard Sparks
Box 32
Dingle, Idaho 83233

J. V. Nolen
302 Meldo Park Dr.
Corpus Christi, Tex. 78411

R. H. Ruana
Box 527
Bonner, Mont. 59823

* George Stone
703 Floyd Rd.
Richardson, Tex. 75080

R. D. Nolen
Rebel Field
Mercedes, Tex. 78570

Russell Knives
See Morseth Knives

Dwight Towell
Rt. 1
Midvale, Idaho 83645

* Robert Ogg
Rt. 1, Box 230
Paris, Ark. 72855

N. H. Schiffman
Box 7373
Murray, Vt. 84107

* Track Knives
1313 2nd St.
Whitefish, Mont. 59937

* John Owens, Jr.
8755 S.W. 96th St.
Miami, Fla. 33156

H. J. Schneider
24296 Via Aquara
Laguna Miguel, Calif. 92677

James Walker
6909 Randolph Macon Dr.
Alexandria, Va. 22301

Ed Pou
322 Cleveland St.
New Albany, Miss. 38652

John J. Schwarz
41–15th Street
Wellsburg, W. Va. 26070

Buster Warenski
Box 214
Richfield, Utah 84701

Ralph Prouty
5240 S.W. 49th Dr.
Portland, Ore. 97405

Corbet Sigman
Star Rt. 1, Box 3
Red House, W. Va. 25168

* Quinton "Red" Watson
612 Olive St.
Upland, Calif. 91786

* Jim Pugh
917 Carpenter St.
Azle, Tex. 76020

Silver Fox Knives
2011 Lenze
La Marque, Tex. 77568

* Weatherford Bros.
4775 Memphis Dr.
Dallas, Tex. 75207

Ray Quincy
Box 1851
Paso Robles, Calif. 93446

Jim Small, Jr.
474 Foster St.
Madison, Ga. 30650

* D. E. Weiler
Box 1576
Yuma, Ariz. 85364

Robt. Whitaker
4633 Berta Rd.
Memphis, Tenn. 38109

* R. W. Wilson
145 Leech St.
Wierton, W. Va. 26026

Bob Wrench
Rt. 5, Box 768
Eugene, Ore. 79402

W. C. Wilber
400 Lucerne Dr.
Spartanburg, S.C. 29302

Art Wiman
Box 92
Plummerville, Ark. 72127

* Don Zaccagnino
Box Zack
Pahokee, Fla. 33476

Gerald Willey
Rt. 1
Greenwood, Del. 19950

Wood Knives
38 So. Venice Blvd.
Venice, Calif. 90291

Richard Zeller
1209 Davis
Fairborn, Ohio 45324

knife etchers
and
engravers

Lynton McKenzie
New Orleans Arms Co., Inc.
240 Rue Chartres
New Orleans, La. 70130

A. A. White Engravers, Inc.
Box 68
Manchester, Conn. 06040

Winston C. Churchill
54 High Street
Ludlow, Vt. 05149

Shaw-Leibowitz
Route 1, Box 421
New Cumberland,
W. Va. 26047

suppliers

For those who may care to try their hand at crafting a knife, a full range of materials and supplies may be obtained from the following:

Indian Ridge Traders
P. O. Box X–50
Ferndale, Mich. 48220

Bob Schrimsher
Custom Knifemaker's Supply
P. O. Box 11448
Dallas, Tex. 75223

Van Sickle Cutlery
Box 3688
San Angelo, Tex. 76901

Knifemaking kits, finished and semi-finished blades and handle materials can be had from:

Dixie Gun Works, Inc.
Union City, Tenn. 38261

Clyde Fischer
Rt. 1, Box 170–M
Victoria, Tex. 77901

Golden Age Arms Co.
Box 82
Worthington, Ohio 43085

Morseth Knives
1705 Highway 71 N
Springdale, Ark. 72764

Randall Made Knives
Box 1988
Orlando, Fla. 32802

Index